High Stakes Selling

By John Blake

Table of Contents

Sales Breakthrough Solutions Resources

Psychometric Tests:

DISC profile:
https://www.tonyrobbins.com/ue/

Gallup strengths finder:
https://www.gallupstrengthscenter.com/Home/en-US/Index

POP Salespeople Selection Profile:
https://www.selfmgmt.com/products/profiles-selection-tools/pop/

Foreword

Before you read this book! For several years now, I've been encouraging my pal John to write a book. Not because I sold him the kit he used to write it, but because I've recognized his talent for closing sales when they count. John and I regularly converse about the sales industry and the state it's in, and I've been on him to get this book done for a while now. The fact that you're reading this means he's done the work and released his genius to the world.

Sales is a game of pressure. You're under pressure to earn commission. You're under pressure to close the prospect. You're applying pressure to the prospect to encourage him or her to make a decision. The pressure in sales only ends the day you retire. Until that day, you'd better get comfortable being under pressure.

When the pressure is high so are the stakes.

Think about it. Everything about sales is high stakes. We literally risk it all in sales. Our income. Our families. Our futures. Everything rises and falls on our ability to close. If those aren't the highest stakes we can face, what is? We put it all on the line for a chance to win big. And we do this every single day.

Sales isn't an undertaking you perfect or master. Every situation is different. Every prospect has their own way of being closed. Even when you use a script, you never have the same sales conversation twice. Sales is a lifelong learning process with a pay plan attached. Your paycheck is a direct reflection of how much value you bring to the marketplace and your ability to handle pressure.

Over the years, I've watched my friend John Blake use sales to improve every area of his life. From earning more income to closing and marrying the woman of his dreams, John has utilized his sales skills in every way possible. John is a living example of someone who's made selling a way of life.

In his book, *High Stakes Selling*, John will teach you how he's used a lifetime of sales experience to rise to the top of the sales industry. He's one of the most knowledgeable people I can think of who's qualified to share such specialized information from experience, not theory.

The lessons you'll learn in this book apply to every area of your life. The stakes are high every day. With death always lurking around the corner, nothing is promised to us. Each day you wake up, the stakes start to climb. With every minute passing by, the stakes get higher. You can use the methods, strategies and tactics you learn from this book in the corporate world as well as at home with your family.

My simple challenge to you is this: as you read this book, plan to use the lessons you'll learn in other areas besides the corporate environment. Sales is a way of life. It's a religion. A belief system. The more you buy in, the more it works for you. Don't limit yourself to just using the information you learn in this book at work. Apply these timely lessons to every area of your life. Make high stakes selling a natural part of your existence.

When the stakes are high, the reward is large. Trust me when I say, "The reward is always worth the risk in sales." The stakes are high as you read this book. You could absorb the information in the following pages and never do a damn thing with it. Or you can learn it, apply it, implement it and it could change your life. You'll never know unless you read on. The stakes have never been higher.

-Ryan Stewman, Founder of Hardcore Closer

Acknowledgments

When you write a book, naturally, you think back on all the people who have helped you to make it possible. This book would never have seen the light of day without my beautiful wife Tanya. Other than my parents, I have never experienced the level of unconditional love, support and encouragement from anyone in my entire life as Tanya has given to me.

Second, I would like to thank the many mentors I have had throughout my career in sales. From Barry and Judy Young, to Leigh Farnell and more recently, Kevin Nations, James Klobassa and Taki Moore.

I also want to thank Ryan Stewman for encouraging me to write this book and for kindly writing the foreword.

In each of your own unique ways, you have shone a light on my path and you have given me invaluable lessons and insights on how to run a successful business.

Third, to my amazing clients both in the action sports industry, and more recently, in service-based and professional advisory businesses, thank you so much for trusting me with the exciting task of helping you to grow your business. It has allowed me to have an absolute ball, while living a business life with the flexibility to navigate some pretty serious storms, so I can lead the lifestyle I absolutely love.

Kind regards,

John Blake

Introduction

I have "contributed" to other sales books before, but have never written my own where I could explain the philosophies, tools and strategies that have helped me, an average high school-educated student get to where I am today in the world of sales. I have been constantly asked by both clients and colleagues when I was going to stop talking about it and simply get it done.

I have also been encouraged and extremely motivated by my wife Tanya (whose sales process I have also helped her work on in her own successful business) to bring my unique take on what is required to succeed in a sales role.

I finally made a commitment to a mastermind group that I became a part of in January, when I told them I would have a book written by September. And up until the first week in September, I hadn't written a single word. (Incidentally, if you ever want to force yourself to write a book, making a promise to people, who will ask you about it, is a great start).

So, with very little time to go before the deadline I had set, I locked in and simply have now gotten it done.

To give every one of my mastermind members a copy of this book will certainly be worthy thanks for their refusal to let me off the hook and hold me accountable until it's completion.

Based on twenty-eight years in sales, twelve years in consulting and five trading under my own name, it's now a reality.

What follows is a collection of high stakes, real-life-in-the-trenches "sales adventures," which have occurred over the last 28 years, and which contain key lessons relating to these experiences. The three pillars and the additional principles I am listing out for you here in this book are each based on the events in my life and have become the foundation of success both for myself and for the business owners and salespeople I have mentored and coached throughout my career.

I hope you both enjoy the ride and receive the lessons you most need to help you along your own path to success, and that they will contribute to the growth of your business as well as give you an edge toward creating success in your own selling efforts and in the greater parts of your life.

Chapter 1

An Unlikely Introduction to Sales

High stakes selling.

The moment you enter the world of business or the world of selling, especially commission-based selling, you will find the stakes to be incredibly high.

You'll even need to be aware of your behavior concerning the sales you don't convert because your conduct is on display, the words you use, the emails you send—every action you exhibit, it all sends a beacon out to the world—either repelling or attracting more, or less business to you.

When you start to consider this, and everything else that rides on your success as a business owner or salesperson, the stakes are incredibly high. At the end of every month, even if you've met your sales target or quota, when the month rolls over, the new month doesn't care. It's game on and last month doesn't matter anymore.

As you gain more success, as you get older and accumulate more responsibility, with more debt and more success to live up to, you'll also find you have a lot more to lose.

Seventeen-Year Old Surfing Fanatic

When I first stumbled unknowingly into the sales world, I was not thinking about becoming a salesperson at all. In fact, I was a 17-year old surfing fanatic. From the time that I was six years old up until I'd begun my sales career, I was (and still am) first and foremost, a surfer.

I was surfing competitively and sponsored by Rip Curl wetsuits. Any spare moment I had was spent thinking about surfing, drawing surfing symbols or illustrations, talking about surfing and of course…actually surfing…

At the time when I began my career in sales, I had just returned from a four-day trip to a place called Denmark in the Southwest of Western Australia. It was around Easter, and I had arrived home from surfing with the Surfboard Riders Club. When I set foot into my house, my mum and dad asked me to come and sit with them in the lounge room.

Now, if in our home, you were ever asked to go and talk to my parents in the lounge room, you knew something serious was going on. As I started walking toward the lounge room, I felt a knot in the pit of my stomach, and a level of nervousness rising within me. I thought I had done something horribly wrong and that my parents had found out about it.

As I racked my brain trying to work out what I might have done wrong that I would be in trouble for, we made our way into the lounge room and sat down. I studied the look on my parents' faces and I noticed it wasn't disappointment I could see. It was pride.

I learned what they wanted to talk to me about was that the guy who was sponsoring me for Rip Curl wetsuits, wanted to meet with me. He had contacted my parents while I was away, and had asked if he could speak to me about the possibility of working for him in his wholesale distribution business.

My parents were absolutely blown away and were flattered with pride at the prospect that my sponsor had called them unsolicited, out of the blue and asked if I would be interested in working for him. I did have a chat with him, and that conversation led to my start in sales at the age of seventeen.

A Car Battery Becomes a Million-Dollar Career

It had been a previous chance encounter that had led up to him making the decision to employ me. I had been at a local petrol station, when he drove his car in to get some fuel. The car I was driving at that time, had broken down and I had organized, prior to his arrival, a new replacement battery.

I had somehow managed to get the service station attendant to agree to install a new battery, without me paying for it at the time and I was just about to drive off. When he asked me, "Are you okay? Do you want a lift anywhere?" I said, as casually as I could, "That's alright. It's sorted." I could see him looking at me, this guy who would eventually ask me to come and work for him and his mind was ticking.

As it turns out, me negotiating a "pay later" arrangement on that replacement battery with the attendant, was the criteria he would use to decide I should work for him.

Oddly enough, throughout our conversation of employment, he at some point, had mentioned the fact I was going to be in sales and my role would involve dealing with clients and selling to them. However, all I heard at the time was, "You're going to get free wetsuits! You're going to get free surf clothing! You're going to get free accessories!" And this…was how I put my toe in the water and was catapulted into the world of sales.

Why I Wrote This Book (AKA Intro Two)

The bigger reason I have written this book however, is because I want to help people who are going into a sales role circumnavigate and avoid a lot of the mistakes that I've made. I've now worked in a sales capacity for 28 years. I have also both coached companies, and many hundreds of salespeople for the last 12 years.

I have seen the long list of things that don't work in sales, and I have also cataloged, developed and refined the shorter list of things that genuinely do work.

What You'll Learn

You'll learn how to have confidence in your actions, in what you say and in how you structure your conversations with existing and potential clients, so you can maximize the amount of sales you extract from every opportunity.

I'll teach you how to help people you work with to achieve the best possible outcome, and how to do it in an efficient way so it serves both you and your client. You'll be able to do this in a manner that's virtually invisible to your client. This philosophy is the backbone of how to create the best outcome with your prospects and clients.

Because it feels invisible to the client, at no point do they ever suspect they're being sold to. This strategy threads all the way through everything you're about to learn in this book.

How It Will Help You

I will encourage you to act on a number of trainings within this book that are designed to cover what it is to be a great salesperson, but also what can contribute to owning and running a thriving sales business. A business that continues to grow, to give you a solid return on your investment in your business, your advertising and your team.

I'm going to share with you, my philosophy on how to understand your numbers. Meaning, what key numbers you need to look at in your data, and what figures you need to shoot for, to grow your sales business.

You'll become aware of how using some specific words…magic words, that when applied to your messages…create specific outcomes and responses. I'm going to share some of those magic words with you, and teach you about the power of stories. How you can use relevant stories to explain about, and sell your special products and services.

Storytelling holds immense power in sales and I will to explain to you why this is true and how you can use this technique to find success in your business.

I'm going to talk to you about the importance of

detachment in the sales process, and how you can progress toward closing a sale without being too attached to the outcome.

And with training, I'm going to share with you several specific training resources that have created millions and millions of dollars' worth of sales for me and my clients.

I'm also going to give you the three core elements on how to find confidence in any sales situation, including high-stakes sales. These core elements can create massive growth in your sales results. And most importantly, how to use them to take responsibility for your situation and results.

I'm going to explain the power of focus and what it can mean for you in terms of taking that leap of faith within your own circumstances. I'll also expand upon the lessons I've learned through various transitions within the different sales businesses I have owned and operated.

I'm going to talk to you about the power of resilience, and how it can serve you when challenges come up, when things inevitably try and stop you in your tracks. I will teach you how you can create your own dream sales business which serves you, one that allows you to operate on your terms, so you can realize the goal of working in the way you desire.

These are my objectives. I'll give you many resources which you can access at: **www.highstakesselling.com**

Here you'll find a specific process and a specific system, which is accessible only to those who have purchased and read this book.

I'm looking forward to sharing these lessons with you. It is my hope that you will use them to build the type of success in your business, in your sales role and in your life of which you have only dreamed.

KEY LESSONS

1. Always remember no matter what you're doing today, your conduct is always on display and you never know who is watching.
2. Your next big opportunity may be only around the corner.

To learn more go to www.highstakesselling.com

Chapter 2

Small Business Sales Apprenticeship

What am I doing at reception school?

One of the first things I had to do in my new role was attend a receptionist course. I'll never forget the day I showed up and walked into the room. It was me and a classroom full of women. At that time, obviously not many guys were answering the phone.

My first task was to answer the phone. I was, in effect, a receptionist—not really what I'd been expecting when I'd said yes to the opportunity—but hey, you've got to start somewhere. So, I was sent to a receptionist course, where I didn't expect to learn much.

We drank cups of tea, and ate cucumber sandwiches and Kingston biscuits. I certainly wasn't anticipating walking out of there with much useful knowledge, and I definitely had no idea that what I would learn that day would be extremely helpful.

In fact, that receptionist course taught me there were specific things you could do, and specific things you could say that could create a vastly different experience for the person on the other end of the phone.

This was my first experience at using distinct combinations of words to create a targeted result and bring about a strategic experience in the person I was having a conversation with.

In effect, receptionists are salespeople and in any sales process, the initial dialogue you have with a new client is crucial...because they are the gateway to your business. The importance of the phone can never be underestimated, especially as it pertains to receptionists.

Asking for More

As I was improving my reception skills, I discovered the importance of asking for more.

The wholesale agency I worked for, sold Rip Curl wet suits and clothing, Quiksilver apparel and a number of other fashion labels. The guy that I worked for sat in the office next to me. At the time, the surf industry was enjoying a large growth curve, so people were ordering a ton of surf wear. In fact, many of the companies in that industry were seeing annual growth in their numbers between 100 and 200 percent.

When each of the orders came through, I could hear my boss pick up the phone. He would call almost every single client, and ask them to order more. He would pick a style, or an area of the range in which they hadn't ordered, then he would ask them to order more.

Some of these people had already bought *100 percent* more than what they had purchased in the previous range, but he wasn't deterred and would often ring them anyway, asking them to take another style. It became a standard procedure; everyone who placed an order, would always receive a call where it was suggested they should order additional product.

My First Sale

During this time, I became more and more confident in my ability on the phone, and therefore, I was given some people to call. My first sale involved simply ringing up a client and suggesting they should order more products than what they had first ordered.

Prior to calling, the process involved going through the orders already placed and assessing what people had ordered, as well as checking out other areas in the range they may have missed. Having listened to my boss do it, I'd memorized what he said, which was a good thing, because suddenly I was the one ringing people up and asking them to order some styles they had potentially missed.

Understanding the Numbers

The couple who ran the wholesale business I worked for at the time, really took me under their wing and taught me some fundamental sales skills. Like how to always look very, very carefully at the numbers. And how to ask for more. As a result, I became pretty accurate at projecting sales numbers that were required to run the business successfully.

I was able to scrutinize the numbers and ratios, to know what percentage of people were ordering what products and oversee carefully, the growth in sales from year-to-year.

To a large extent, we dealt with a fixed number of accounts, but the amount that each client ordered was monitored closely to make sure we were continually encouraging growth for those accounts from season to season.

It's critical on every order you receive to assess it and ensure no stone has been left unturned, and that every single opportunity has been maximized.

Over time, I learned how to sell. I also became quite proficient in the numbers part of the business. In addition to learning how to sell, I was also taught how to balance the books in our wet suit stock account.

Learning the numbers side of the business, I would come to learn in later years, would serve me extremely well when it came to running my own business.

Understanding the numbers is crucial. If you don't know what your numbers are from day to day, from week to week, from year to year, it's going to be exceedingly difficult to grow a business.

To quote well-known consultant Peter Drucker, "What gets measured gets managed."

Unless you have specific revenue numbers you are shooting for, unless you know what your average transaction size is, unless you know what your conversion rates are, it will be difficult for your business to prosper.

Becoming crystal clear on what those numbers are and looking at the activities and the behaviors underpinning them is crucial to maintaining growth in a sales business.

I also learned 20 percent of people will generally choose a premium version of your product or service if you offer it, which is a massive untapped opportunity for many businesses.

Making sure that you've got some clear parameters around what you're shooting for on a daily, weekly, monthly, quarterly and yearly basis is the foundation for growing sales in any organization.

In the next chapter, you'll learn how I sold my first million dollars in sales in one year.

Chapter 3

Driving Around Lost...All Day

The time I was thrown in at the deep end.

After working for the surf wholesale business in Perth for four years, I was asked to join one of the companies I had been representing in Western Australia, over in Sydney. I was 21 and had never lived anywhere but Perth and at the time it felt like a huge move, uprooting my entire existence, jumping on an airplane and moving there.

I was now working for a national distributor selling Morey Boogie Bodyboards and No Fear Clothing. My boss was a big, friendly Tongan bloke called George.

This was my induction: "Here are the keys to the car downstairs and here's your range of bodyboards that we want you to sell. You have the entire territory of New South Wales," of which there were around 150 to 200 clients.

Additionally: "Here's an account list with all the people we want you to sell this range to and your road directory," (because in those days there was no such thing as a GPS.) "Off you go." And that was it.

Selling My First Million

Fast forward 12 months. I had sold my first million dollars' worth of product. And I had narrowly escaped around 10 or 15 accidents, because driving in New South Wales is quite different than driving around in Perth, which by comparison, is a small country town. The roads are a lot more dangerous. There are more cars to steer around, and it was a perilous place to be a sales rep.

Having sold a million dollars' worth of products, I had become acutely aware of the power of my words. Specific instances where knowing the right things to say in certain situations were very powerful.

For example, once, when I arrived at a sports store to show the buyer a range of bodyboards, I found the person who had been on the road prior to me had made a lot of promises to them that were not followed up on and fulfilled.

The Power of Magic Words

I remember on this particular occasion, listening to the buyer go on for at least half an hour, telling me all the things the previous rep had done wrong and all the promises he had made that hadn't been delivered on.

I had recently read about an approach to dealing with issues such as this and for clients who have been left unimpressed by a predecessor you have taken over from. So, I began using this tactic I had read about with this guy. Without interruption, I allowed him to speak freely and openly. The client told me, "Your predecessor did this. He did that. He didn't do this. He was terrible at this. He left us in a lurch on this. He didn't follow up on this." I let this guy talk on and explain exactly what it was that he was upset about.

At the end, I said to him, "If you were the person in charge of the company, and you had somebody who was doing a job like that and representing the brand like that, what would you do?" The client replied, "I'd get rid of them." I said, "And that's exactly what they've done."(big smile.)

To my surprise, it instantly diffused and shut down that argument. Simply going through the process and asking him that question had totally defused the situation, which left the road clear to show him a range and take a substantial order that was bigger than what he had ever ordered previously. And I was able to move on with my day.

Because of my predecessors' unfulfilled promises, I had to figure out how to deal with many buyers who were very unhappy with Morey Boogie, the brand I sold, and turn their experience into a positive one.

I learned that strategy from a Tom Hopkins book, *How to Master the Art of Selling*. It was an effective example of the power of words—the power of magic words—if you will. As you read further into this book, I will explain more about the power of words and how they can work for you.

"That'll Do, PAL!!"

Another interesting example of this type of situation occurred when I visited a large sports shop, and the guy who owned the place was a very famous, very big, burly rugby league player. He bought mostly sports product.

We specialized in product for surf shops, and product for sports stores. I'd gone through and shown him our range and he'd picked three or four different boards as well as some flippers. As I was writing out his order, I casually asked him, "Do you think this is going to be enough?" Usually my magic words to increase an order.

He looked over at me, and said, "That'll do, PAL!!" He was such an intimidating fellow. To even have had the courage to ask him such a question was bold. When he said, "That'll do, PAL!!" it came out in a stern but playful way, but it was an interesting example of the fact that, yeah, there are magic words that work, but they don't always work 100 percent of the time.

The main lesson here, of course, is to ask. Because if you don't ask, the answer is already "no."

One of the trainings on my website goes into the process of scripting. Feel free to check it out at **www.highstakesselling.com.**

Headhunted

At the end of that period, I was headhunted. What came next would be the most exciting journey I had encountered yet in my career, where I would help take a business from almost bankrupt to a multi-million dollar-success story for the whole of Australia, Asia and New Zealand.

KEY LESSONS

1. Words can be powerful tools if used properly.
2. Always ask – if you don't the answer is already no.
3. 20 percent of any market will choose a premium version of what you sell if you offer it.
4. Get to know and closely monitor closely your key numbers

To learn more go to www.highstakesselling.com

Chapter 4

From $750K to $6.5M in Three Years

Previous to finishing up with the bodyboarding company, I had had an in-depth conversation with a gentleman I'd known since my teens. He ran the Australian distributorship for a sunglass company.

The Locks are About to Be Changed

In my initial discussions with him and his accountant, I had learned the company was not doing well. He had the distributorship rights for Australia as well as Asia and New Zealand and his company was using a method of finance called factoring. This was a process whereby an invoice is raised and a finance company would pay 75 to 80 percent of the value of that invoice before the customer had paid. The finance company then takes a commission from the other 20–25 percent upon payment by the customer.

This way of financing a business allowed the company to buy more stock, pay their staff and have better cash flow. Because his business was performing poorly, the factoring company was threatening to change the locks, repossess the stock and send everybody home unless their sales improved significantly.

The meeting I walked into was a crisis session. At this stage, some of their biggest accounts had pulled their business and were no longer dealing with them. His company was in seriously bad shape.

Part-Time 22-Year-Old National Sales Manager

The agreement we made that day was, I would be the national sales manager, I would work for three days of the week and my wage to begin would be $250 cash per week. I would work for them Monday, Tuesday and Wednesdays. On Thursday, Friday, Saturday and Sundays, I would run a small graphic design business from home, which was another daring move.

After our discussion, I'd walked into a computer store and bought $12,000 worth of graphic design gear, to start a graphic design studio, which I had wanted to do since I left school. In the early 90's $12,000 was a massive amount of money.

In my new role as National Sales Manager for the sunglass company, the business had begun to improve substantially. There was one big opportunity I immediately saw with the company not dealing with three major surf shops in Australia.

Three Phone Calls Worth Three Million Bucks

My first goal was to get those accounts on board. Before I reached out to anyone, I researched exactly who it was that I needed to access to open the accounts, then down to the most granular detail, their biggest objection. Since the company couldn't fly me to them, I had to get on the phone.

In three telephone calls, I established sunglass accounts that would go on to be worth in excess of three million dollars per year. At 22, I already understood the power of getting on the phone and asking for business.

The Power of Scripting

Within three and a half years, we had grown sunglass sales from $750,000 to $6.5 million per year throughout Australia, Asia and New Zealand. And we had done this largely by landing bigger retailers. We engineered a specific conversation to have with the key decision makers in those businesses, and in doing so, ensured we would make it easy for them to say yes.

I've created a webinar that walks you through how to craft your own conversation, and you can access it at this link: **www.highstakesselling.com.**

The Power of Stories

I also became aware that the power of stories could make a massive difference during the sales process.

At the time, the biggest sunglass company around was Oakley. Oakley was very sport and traditional. It was corporate and clean, but a bit sterile.

The story we told that seemed to resonate with our retailers, concerned the man who started the eyewear company whose product we sold. He had been one of the main designers at Oakley, and he had left Oakley to start his own sunglass company in his garage.

He had been a frustrated military guy. All he'd ever wanted was to be in the Army or the Air Force. The story goes that he had hoped to make it into the Air Force, but they hadn't accepted him because he was colorblind. In any case, he had a pretty inarguable reason as to why he hadn't been able to join the Armed Forces.

So, he wound up as this kind of mad wanna-be military guy. After he had left Oakley, he would sit in his garage and come up with unique wrap around designs that were made popular by Lenny Kravitz and Madonna and had this ultra-grungy, underground rock 'n' roll feel.

This happened around the time Nirvana was popular. People were into grunge and it resonated with many of them. As we were expanding the range, we would tell the story about the company and how it was created in San Clemente in this guy's garage when he had left Oakley, and he had come up with these three styles that had exploded onto the market and which became incredibly popular.

When I run my online and live trainings I take clients through what I call the stories exercise which allows clients to create powerful, persuasive stories about their company and the products and services they sell. To access this training on the power of stories and the worksheet where you can create your own powerful stories to use when you are selling simply go to www.highstakesselling.com

At one point, Coca-Cola's marketing company even contacted us. They wanted to purchase 28,000 pairs of a certain style we sold because in their market research, they'd realized the most popular brand in their target audience, which was 18 to 24-year-olds, was the brand we were selling. They envisioned running a competition, and so were hoping to purchase 28,000 pairs of this style. It was a powerful time for the brand.

One of the things that made a difference in our company's success during this time, was making sure we gave the employees access to strong and proven sales systems. I'm going to talk specifically about the power of training your team and how to implement these systems in the next chapter.

The business grew so quickly within the three and a half years I was there as national sales manager, that the owner was able to negotiate the sale of the Southeast Asia distributorship for a substantially large sum.

In the next chapter, I'll reveal some of the strategies and training that underpinned the growth that allowed us to go from $750K to $6.5 million at a lightning fast rate.

KEY LESSONS

1. Designing your sales conversations using specific phraseology can transform your sales results.
2. Using stories strategically in your sales conversations with clients is the most powerful way to sell anything

To learn more go to www.highstakesselling.com

Chapter 5

Million Dollar Training

Training: Two of the Three Things That Made the Biggest Difference

Over those three years, a lot of people asked me, "How were you able to grow the business so quickly? How were you able to get from $750,000 to $6.5 million in three years?" It's a great question. Essentially, three things made the biggest difference.

The first one was that we had a top-notch product that flew out of retailers' shops. That was a given, and it's a critical piece of the sales puzzle to have in place to ensure you experience thriving success. But it was the other two things that made the biggest difference, above the product quality and mystique.

The second irreplaceable sales element was that we made sure we trained our reps on how to help retailers make more money out of sunglasses. When I first started in the sunglass market, very few people made cabinets to assist retailers in selling more sunglasses.

So, we created sunglass cabinets that looked fantastic...freestanding, head-high sunglass display cases that allowed retailers to showcase more product.

At that time, we had the volume to substantiate retailers carrying a hefty stock of sunglasses, so they could justify putting these big cabinets in their stores.

We were helping them make more money out of displaying our sunglasses in their stores, through giving them the correct way to display the product, which enabled them to have more on display. The more sunglasses on display, the more they would sell. In short order, we trained our reps to help retailers create more money out of their sunglass inventory.

We also trained the reps on how to maximize their sales by creating conversations they could have with their retailers on a regular basis, which in effect, helped to maximize the stock turns for the retailer. This training was all about assisting the retailer in moving as much sunglass product out of their stores as they possibly could.

Teaching Kids how to Sell Sunglasses

The final piece of the sales puzzle was taking the time to train the floor staff on how to sell sunglasses to the general public. It was innovative thinking, because at that point, there weren't many people focusing on this initiative.

The average person working in a surf shop was between 16 and 19 years old. In most cases, they were female and fresh out of school. The sunglass category itself was also relatively fresh back then. So, there wasn't a ton of knowledge around eyewear.

Since the floor staff didn't know how to sell sunglass product, we needed to help them. We trained them on how to deal with the public when they walked into the store—how to approach them, how to work out what sunglasses would suit various faces, etc.

We showed them the type of face shapes that should be matched with certain kinds of sunglass frames for the most flattering result and how to sell the benefits of the various lenses we had in the range. This had an exponential effect on the way the product was working in the store.

The multiplier effect of having more products on display, of having our reps service each of the retail stores more regularly and more productively, plus, training up the floor staff responsible for selling the product on how to sell sunglasses more effectively to the public, had this accelerator effect on our sales.

My Own Training

In addition to the three keys, which were largely responsible for our exponential growth, I also brought an advantage to our success with my own training. In both the role I had with the sunglass company and the role I had with the bodyboarding company, even though I'd been given product training, I hadn't been provided sales training. Because of this, as I was figuring out the elements to increase growth, I was also devouring dozens and dozens of sales books. I was going to sales seminars. I was listening to sales audios.

I was refining my own skills and passing my self-taught knowledge onto our reps for them to use within their roles. I translated all the different training I was doing to fit the conversations we would have with our retailers and the conversations the staff would have with the public walking in and buying our product.

In sales, it is critical to continually invest in yourself through the purchase of sales books, training, mentoring and seminars. Learn from the experts in your field to grow your own understanding and success.

I was using my newfound info to train my team on how to sell effectively to the retail stores, and teaching the teams working on the floor, how to sell the product successfully. This training became a massive part of our company's success.

One of the highlights during this exciting time, involved a huge eyewear account. Their stores weren't categorized as surf shops and so, they differed from the majority of my clients. My predecessor had had two or three meetings with the lady who was the buyer and in every meeting, they had reached deadlock, which is a negotiation term for "no deal." The conversation would get to a certain point, and then both parties would walk away from the table with no agreement in place.

I had arranged a meeting with this lady and as I left the office my boss casually said, "Good luck. I doubt very much you'll get anywhere with her." I was still very young, about 22 when I met this woman and with such a negative rap, I was a little apprehensive about this meeting. Things were going okay, when in the middle of conversation, she said, "Are you dealing with Sunglass Hut?" (a competitor of theirs.)

We weren't dealing with Sunglass Hut then. So, I said, "No. We're not." When she asked why we weren't, I said, "Because we don't want to work with Sunglass Hut right now." She then said, "You should be careful." And when I asked why, she told me legally we couldn't not supply them. To which I replied, "Yes, we can, we can choose who we want to deal with."

We'd had a very cordial conversation up until that point about the possibility of this eyewear chain stocking our sunglasses, but suddenly, the conversation took a turn for the worse. We had now devolved into a hypothetical, legal conversation about consumer law and whether we should be supplying (hypothetically) another account in the market.

I had the presence of mind before the conversation had degenerated further to the point of no return, to stop mid-conversation and raise both of my hands in a gesture of *I give up*. There I was, just looking at her with this semi-stupid expression on my face with my hands held up in front of me in a gesture of conceding.

In truth, it was more a gesture of *why are we even talking about this*? I didn't say anything more as I raised my hands, and intuitively stopped the conversation, shrugging at the same time, while holding eye contact with her. No exaggeration; we sat in silence for about three or four minutes staring at each other.

The next thing I knew, we were mapping out an opening order of sunglasses for this national eyewear chain, which operated over 200 stores. This would go on to become an account for many years, worth millions of dollars. Selling to that woman, is to this day, one of the strangest experiences I have ever had resulting in the closing of one of the most profitable sales I have been involved in to date.

The lesson to take from this story centers around the concept of detachment. When we get to a point in a sale where we're too attached to the outcome, we find ourselves in danger of losing the sale. In this situation, I was prepared to walk out, but I also held my ground. I was looking at her as if to say, *this is pretty irrelevant to our conversation. Are we going to work together on this or not?*

Detachment and dismissal from, or refusal to engage in something irrelevant and petty, was the factor that made the difference.

In the next chapter, I tell how I left that business and moved back to Perth, and how I applied these lessons to launch my own successful company.

KEY LESSONS

1. Detachment from the outcome of a sales conversation makes your product more attractive to a potential client.
2. Just like in sports, getting the right sales training will help you to get to the top of your industry and your earning potential.

To learn more go to www.highstakesselling.com

Chapter 6

Starting My Own Sales Business, Leaping into the Abyss

Prior to moving back to Perth from Sydney, I had been contributing to the success of others by building up their businesses, training their sales teams and increasing my employer's wealth. It was time to take a leap of faith into my own business.

Mambo Interview

At that exact time, by chance, one of my colleagues who was the sales manager for Mambo, contacted me, and said, "Do you know anyone—because I know you're from Perth—that you think would be a good agent for us in Western Australia? We're about to get rid of our agent there, and we are interested in finding someone really good to represent our brand as a wholesaler."

My initial response was, "No I'm sorry, I can't think of anybody at this particular time, but if I do, I'll come back to you."

As soon as I hung up the phone however, I became more and more convinced that the agent they were looking for could be me. I felt like I had achieved what I'd set out to at the sunglass company, and I'd decided it might be time, after living in Sydney for four years, to move back to Perth.

So, I rang the sales manager back, and said, "Look, I've been thinking about the question you asked me, and there's someone I know who would be very good." When he said, "Who's that?" I said, "Me."

The next thing I knew, I was sitting in a meeting with the two owners of Mambo being asked *what would you do if we told you that you had the agency rights for Mambo for WA?*

I replied, "If you told me that I had the agency for WA, I would resign tomorrow from my current employment."

"I would then give notice on the place I'm renting, pack up all my stuff and move back to Perth. I reckon I could be set up and ready to go with your new range within two weeks." Even as I said it, I had absolutely no idea whether I could actually pull off what I was promising to them.

The next day, the sales manager from Mambo called, and said, "Look, it's yours. I'll send you a Letter of Appointment. All you need to do is reply to that letter accepting our offer, and then you can move back to West Australia." Suddenly everything that I had said, was happening.

I gave notice to the sunglass company, which was now under new ownership having been sold for millions. I then told my girlfriend, who had no idea what was happening, gave notice to the place I was renting and moved back to Perth, and into my parents' place. I found an office and showroom, and true to my word, was set up and ready to go with the new range within two weeks.

In two weeks, I literally changed my entire life. I'd gone from earning in 1996, $90,000 a year, which was a lot of money, not only for a 25-year-old, but it was just a lot of money period; to taking on an agency worth $500,000 a year in sales, that was only worth a measly $35,000 in commission.

In other words, I was working for a brand with a net total commission of $35,000 per year for the entire state of WA.

Obviously, I had recognized big potential within the Mambo brand, and I had the confidence to believe I could build it back up to its potential. In addition, I secured a second brand for my agency to wholesale with Vans sneakers, and true to my word, in two weeks, was set up and operating as the new West Australian agent for Mambo and Vans Shoes.

The Mambo ranges were consistently good. It wasn't long before I was able to massively increase sales. In West Australia, Mambo sales went from

$500,000 a year to two million dollars a year within three years.

When I started that wholesale business, I had very little capital, probably about $20,000 in savings. Plus, when you start an agency, you don't get paid for many months. I was a commission-only wholesaler, and I didn't get a retainer.

The Bouncer Who Never Hit Anyone

I didn't receive a commission check for close to 10 months, so I worked as a bouncer at night whilst establishing my business to pay for some of my expenses.

Luckily, they've changed the laws regarding commissions since that time. Now, a business is required to pay an advance on commissions but back in 1996, I had no income whatsoever.

I remember rocking up to my first night as a bouncer at one of Perth's busiest and most popular night clubs. A big, thickset Asian guy I was working with, said to me, "Do you train?"

I asked him if he meant to ask me if I was some kind of karate expert, because he certainly appeared as though he might be. He said, "No." And I replied, "That's good because I'm not." He went on to say, "Look, all I want to know is are you fit?" I told him

I was.

Interestingly, as a bouncer, I was able to use the sales, negotiation and influencing skills I had to avoid getting in fights and to break them up. As a result, I never threw anyone out and I never entered into a fight myself. My sales skills really helped to diffuse many potentially volatile situations without ever having to hit anyone.

I remember the actual day I received the first commission check that covered all my monthly overheads for the business. I opened the envelope and looked at it. It was made out for20 grand. In my other hand, I held my mobile phone. I dialed the number of the night club and told the manager I would no longer be working there, which was a hugely satisfying thing to do because I definitely didn't want to be a bouncer for the rest of my life.

You Can Make Anything Work if You Want It Badly Enough

What I had learned through this process is that it's tremendously satisfying to start up your own business and focus on the main recipient of that business—you. I had to make a lot of sacrifices, like living back in my old room in my parents' house and not going out socially.

I didn't have money to spend on clothes, drinking,

to go to dinners, or any of those types of things. I was too busy working insanely hard as my own boss. I was still only twenty-six

What I realized from that time in my life, is that you can make anything work if you focus on it and if you want it enough. Many people thought I was nuts to walk away from a high-powered, high-paying job, and move back to West Australia, taking on the agency for a brand only generating $35,000 in commissions.

But through persistence, and the consistent growth of Mambo and the other brands I had taken on, I built gross sales within my agency to over two million, which now meant I was earning over $200,000 per year in commissions. For an agent in West Australia, having doubled and tripled the sales in my business, I had achieved what I'd wanted to in a short time—essentially, over three years and before the age of thirty.

Whether you take a leap of faith and go into your own business or move out of your comfort zone within your employment, it is essential to take chances and to continue progressing within your sales career as if you stay where it is comfortable you will never know what great opportunities await you.

In the next chapter, you'll learn how easy it is to

take your eye off the ball and how I went from being a commission-generating machine to a world-class whinger.

KEY LESSONS

1. You can make anything happen if you want it enough and are prepared to give it your 100-percent focus.
2. Be prepared to bite off more than you can chew sometimes; you will be surprised at what you can achieve when the heat is on.

To learn more go to www.highstakesselling.com

Chapter 7

Becoming the World's Biggest Whinger

After eight years of running my agency, and successfully growing the labels I represented, some by 200, 300, 400 percent and generating in excess of over two million dollars a year in sales and over $200,000 a year in commissions, some attitudes were changing toward the action sports industry.

One, it had reached its peak, and had begun its decline. It had had many years of organic growth, to the point where the industry had matured. A lot of the biggest brands had floated on the stock exchange and were now being run by people with short-term visions focused on how to deliver increased shareholder returns as opposed to growing a sustainable business capable of standing the test of time.

Mambo fell into this category. They had been bought out by the company manufacturing the majority of their apparel. This company was, in fact, the biggest manufacturer of apparel in the Southern Hemisphere. They had a huge business with department stores.

Mambo was a unique brand that had embodied a delicate mix of culture and art, and had a dedicated and discerning following. When a company is sold, there are always a couple of predictable events that will generally happen. The first one is the existing management normally will stay on in a managerial capacity as part of the buyout.

When this takes place, you are usually told, "Don't worry. Nothing's going to change. It's business as usual." When you hear those words, what you can expect is, a lot of changes are about to go down. And that was exactly what happened. For a start, just as it had developed in the sunglass company when it had been sold, four or five people were now in charge of making decisions. The decisions that were now being made were being made for different reasons than the past had dictated.

It's All Their Fault

Whereas, the original owners of Mambo had been making decisions based on what was best for the brand and what they were passionate about, the new owners—having paid over $20 million for the brand—were making choices on what would generate the most return in the quickest possible amount of time.

Because of those three key factors: the company had changed hands, the industry had taken a downward turn for the worse and there was a scattered decision-making process at play, the business began to change. The first shock came in the form of deleting the two strongest selling items in the range—the two responsible for approximately 50 percent of Mambo's annual sales.

Because of this, within six months, sales across the board had been reduced by 50 percent. This had a huge effect on me as Mambo was my biggest brand. I had a large amount of exposure.

My idea to resolve this problem involved me jumping on an airplane, flying to Sydney and airing my grievances to the new owners. So, I did just that. I explained to them the things I was concerned about. Like any big company, they listened, but they didn't, (and as it turned out couldn't) really do anything about it.

Because my concerns weren't taken seriously, I started becoming resentful towards the brand. I started blaming the brand for the fact I was not getting the results I wanted and for the fact my agency had begun moving backwards. I had recently relocated from my original premises into a larger 200-square meter office and showroom. I had staff. I had an expensive company car and a commercial lease that had jacked my outgoings considerably, so I had a lot to lose.

It was an emotional time for me, but the overarching way I dealt with my feelings was to simply blame

Mambo and put fault into what they were doing. The other brands I represented were performing well, but Mambo, the central pillar of my business, had been the one delivering the most income.

During that trying time, I would literally whinge or complain to anybody who would listen. This went on for a while. I would tell anyone and everyone how business was going and how badly Mambo was now running everything. How wrong they were. How they were ruining the brand. How it was becoming more and more untenable. I would then tell them the fashion ranges being released were terrible.

My "Give Yourself an Uppercut" Moment

It was my wife at the time, who said to me, "Do you realize you have been whinging about this for a year?" It was one of those "give yourself an uppercut" moments where I felt like a big mirror had been held up in front of me. I immediately realized she was 100 percent right.

I had complained endlessly to anybody who would listen, and I had taken absolutely no responsibility whatsoever for the situation. So, I flipped it and took responsibility. Just like that, and by doing so, I realized I had a highly-respected wholesale agency in my hands. Meaning, I was an independent wholesaler, I could choose to take on any brand I wanted to. My business didn't revolve around Mambo.

I had allowed my business to become too reliant on one brand. So much so, that I had left myself vulnerable to its popularity receding. I had been exposed. At any point, I could have changed that situation. I could have gone out and found a different range to represent. I could have turned the situation around.

Instead, I caught the disease of blame. It's an insidious disease, because the more righteous you become, the more passionate you become, and subsequently, the more blind you become to the responsibility you need to take.

The shift that took place was quite profound, I realized what I needed to do was change the way I thought about my own business. In fact, I remember it clearly. In the moment I took responsibility, I thought to myself, *I can change this. I can just find other brands to represent and start to develop those brands*, and then my situation turned around. My mindset changed instantly. And my confidence returned.

I almost felt like getting on the phone and ringing up every single person I had complained to, to tell them I was sorry for being a whinger!

Bulletproof Confidence in Selling

The big lesson from this experience is that if you want to be 100 percent congruent in sales, everything you say must be aligned with the way your voice sounds and the way your body is presented; this makes you as convincing as possible. To accomplish congruency, three elements need to be in place.

The first element concerns how you feel about yourself. You need to have confidence in your ability and confidence in the way you feel about yourself.

The second piece that needs to be in alignment is confidence in your product.

To use the example we've been talking about with Mambo, I was no longer confident in the product. I wasn't confident the product I was selling to my retailers was going to sell through and that they were going to get a good return on it.

The third thing you need to have confidence in is the company you represent.

As a salesperson, this is true. As a business owner, this is true. Unless these three things are in total alignment, unless you are at the 100-

percent level with the way you feel about yourself, the way you feel about your product and the way you feel about the company you represent, then your ability to sell will be severely compromised.

Taking Responsibility

This was a critical lesson to learn. If I hadn't come to the realization I needed to take responsibility for my own situation, I could very well have gone bankrupt, as I also had a few properties to maintain. I had a new wife who wasn't working and who was pregnant. I had car leases, and lots of overheads and exposure. In that moment, when I took responsibility, my life began to transform.

The business started to transform as well. It began to recover. I picked up a brand of footwear called Havaianas—a range of thongs taking the industry by storm. Massive amounts of Havaianas were being sold globally.

At the same time, I met the person who would soon become my business partner. We began talking about the possibility of creating a business, which would center on helping other businesses in the surf industry to increase their results. The timing for this opportunity was perfect.

In the next chapter, I reveal how I turned my

experiences and successes in the surf and action sports industries into a consulting business that would eventually be worth millions of dollars in fees—as well as hundreds of millions in business growth for the companies I consulted to.

KEY LESSONS

1. The moment you assign blame, you make something or someone else responsible for your success or failure.
2. Taking responsibility gives you power, momentum and opens up infinite possibilities.
3. In order to sell effectively, you must have bulletproof confidence in yourself, your product and the company you represent.

To learn more go to www.highstakesselling.com

Chapter 8

Jumping on the Rocket

After having a successful business that had gone backward and then taking full responsibility for fully turning it around, I began to see bigger possibilities for myself.

I was again achieving great success in my business when I had an encounter with a gentleman while playing water polo. Through a mutual friend, he'd found out I had previously fronted a band and he emailed me, asking me to come and sing at a club function. Unfortunately, I couldn't make it on the date they had set for the event but as I looked at the email, I noted in the signature, he had included a link to his website. So, I clicked on it. He was a certified professional speaker, which meant he had spoken at more than 300 speaking engagements. As a corporate coach and consultant, he had been operating in that space for over 20 years.

I phoned him to tell him I wouldn't be able to perform at the singing gig. I also said, "I had a look at your website, and what you do seems like a lot of fun." He replied, "Are you interested in that sort of thing?" He then invited me to have a chat with him about it. Shortly afterwards, we met for a cup of coffee.

Surf Industry Sales Coach

As it turns out, my next opportunity was sitting right under my nose. I would soon become a coach, mentor and consultant for many of the companies I had previously worked for, or encountered in my 18 years in the surfing industry.

Having worked in Western Australia, dealing with all the different surf and action sports retailers there, having held the position of national sales manager in Sydney, and having connected with all the action sports retailers in the whole of the Australian, Asian and New Zealand region, I was now in a unique place to set up a niche-specific sales and business development company based around the surf industry.

No one at the time had thought of doing this, and there wasn't anybody in WA, or Australia, operating with the same industry background, level of experience and the same unique skill set I now possessed.

So, Blue Rocket Consulting was established. I went from, again, having a comfortable existence in my wholesale business, to taking another leap into an entirely new business and starting again.

The idea to help retailers sell more product had been

born from hours and hours of standing in retail stores waiting for the owner to finish up with whatever he was doing so that I could show him a range of clothing, or wet suits, or shoes. I had watched countless numbers of customers walk into those stores, not be greeted or given assistance and then watched them turn around and walk out without buying a thing.

I saw a promising opportunity to establish a business helping retailers increase their sales by exposing missed opportunities to connect and convert these customers into store clients.

My first clients were some of the same people in the sunglass industry I had originally instructed in staff training sessions on how to sell to the public. These were the exact businesses that were now inviting me back to work on a sales system that they would then use to train existing and new staff.

For a year, I ran both the wholesale business, which was thriving again, and the consulting business. I used a lot of the training and personal development work I had absorbed from my consulting business to run my agency more efficiently and close sales faster.

In my first year as a consultant, I earned a six-figure income doing it part time. Even better was the fact that it was the most fun I had ever had in business.

I was helping people to do things at a much more accelerated rate than the numerous years I had spent making hundreds and hundreds of mistakes to become an expert in my field.

I was helping my clients to shorten their learning curve, in some cases by years, so they could implement the same things, get measurable results, using a proven, more efficient sales process—and this was all happening within two or three months of starting our coaching program.

The Most Fun Ever in Business

I couldn't believe how lucrative this new business was and I was having an absolute ball helping the retailers. Some of the wholesalers heard what I was up to, and suddenly, I found myself working with surf wholesale businesses, too.

Companies like Oakley, O'Neil, Rusty and Ripcurl, some of the biggest brands in the country and in the world, were now inviting me to train their salespeople.

After the first 12 months, I realized I was infinitely more passionate about the consulting business than the fashion agency. So, I closed the fashion agency and went full time into the consulting business at the start of 2005.

Teaching the Americans to Sell

One of the highlights in those early years of consulting was being flown over to America to train 110 domestic sunglass reps for Electric Sunglasses on how to become more effective agents. Teaching the Americans how to sell was a huge boost to my business, a huge boost to my confidence and a lot of fun...it helped that the people who had started Electric were the same people who had operated the sunglass company I'd worked for as the national sales manager.

It was fantastic to go back and rekindle a lot of those old relationships and to add value in a totally different way.

Massive Personal and Client Breakthroughs

During this period, I experienced incredible personal and client breakthroughs, which were fueled by the combination of my successful partnership and the rise in selling consulting. Our fees were rocketing up quickly at the time, selling $70,000 year-long programs to some of the country's largest businesses.

In time, we moved into different industry types besides the surfing field. We took on companies in telecommunications, real estate and in many other industries. These clients wanted our expertise to ensure their salespeople developed the right tools, strong confidence and the ability to convert increased sales in a more systematic way.

During this time, I married and we had moved down south to Margaret River. Having always been a passionate surfer, I was living my dream life. I was working with dream clients I loved, doing work I loved and having a bigger blast in business than I had ever had in my entire 20-year career. Running a business, being 100 percent autonomous and winning exciting consulting projects with all sorts of different companies was quite the sweet spot.

My Dream Life

My dream life was living in Margaret River, a three-minute walk to the beach, surfing whenever I wanted or at least, when I was at home, and a family, which now included my young daughter Mischa.

At that point, things were going ridiculously well. Little did I know a massive storm was brewing. Soon, you'll read about how my life crashed down around me in the most devastating way possible.

KEY LESSON

1. The moment you make a strong commitment to something, possibilities and opportunities begin to expand in front of you.

To learn more go to www.highstakesselling.com

Chapter 9

Breaking Through the Traditional Consulting Model

When I started consulting 12 years ago, there were fewer coaches and consultants in the industry.

Fast forward to the present, and you have all sorts of different companies pumping out "qualified coaches" and "consultants."

Back then, the traditional consulting model was typically, that of a speaker. You would speak at an event. You would speak at a conference. You would register with a speaker's bureau.

A lot of the business would come through the speaker's bureau, so you would present at a conference, and then get additional work leading on from the gig. The gentleman I was in partnership with, had, used that same model.

When you spoke at a conference, the assumption was that, (in terms of what I was doing: sales) somehow a one-off 90-minute keynote or 2-hour presentation—after lunch, when everybody had just had a whole bunch of steak and chips, and their blood sugar levels were crashing—would magically transform sales teams into masterful salespeople.

Of course, that's not the case. If you want to get better at anything, you need multiple exposures to the same material; you need coaching; you need support and you need the process of ongoing improvement. Using that model, you would speak at a conference and maybe one or two follow up sessions...and *that* would be primarily it.

Going from Selling Single Days of Consulting to $40K, $50K and $70K Packages

The first year I was in partnership, I did this exercise, where I'd go back and look at the list of everyone we had worked with. I cut and pasted all the people out of our accounting software package, and then I popped them into an Excel spreadsheet.

I ranked them, from the highest fee-paying client we had, all the way down to the lowest fee-paying client, and I came up with 75 clients. At the top, were some relatively big clients, people who were spending $60,000, $70,000 and $80,000 with us per year. In the middle, as you might assume, were middle-sized ones and down at the bottom, were some really small ones.

I then highlighted the second half of the 75 on that list, that either myself or my business partner had dealt with and pressed "Delete." When I looked at the new bottom line, I had an epiphany.

Essentially, the shift in the bottom line was no more than 11 percent. **When I removed half of the business we had done, it only made an 11 percent difference to the bottom line**.

I realized we could have done half the work, and it would have made little or no difference to the amount of overall business we were transacting. The other epiphany was, we would have more time to help clients that were investing the most with us as well as have the time to focus on researching and approaching other key clients to engage our services. It was a colossal realization.

Longer Term Engagements

In that moment, and in future meetings, we decided we were only going to work with clients on a yearly basis. We realized the clients who had achieved the best results were those who had worked with us over a longer period of time, who'd had multiple exposures to our coaching.

Bundling Our Services

The next question was, "Okay. How are we going to go from selling single days of consulting to selling $40,000, $50,000, $60,000 and $70,000 packages?"

We made the decision almost overnight to simply

bundle our services into a 12-month Sales and Business Transformation Program.

We had program options that went from $20,000 to $70,000. After talking to people about our programs, we found the majority of people chose the $30,000 option.

Before long, we discontinued the $20,000 package.

When we changed our offer from daily to yearly programs, our average client transaction size went from $7,000 to $30,000 per year, almost overnight, simply through deciding definitively how we were going to operate. We evolved from selling one-day packages to marketing and selling premium consulting packages. It was an immense shift that caused a huge change in our results.

Over the next two years, not only were we able to grow our business, but we used the lessons we had learned to help many other businesses bundle their products and services.

Premium Consulting Services

In the newly designed programs, we mentored and serviced our clients closely, and provided valuable and profitable services to them, which in turn, caused tremendous breakthroughs in their business.

It was a successful seven years and a highly successful partnership. Blue Rocket had not only spawned a shift in our business model, but had allowed us to explode our results in both the income we were generating and in the results we were producing for our clients.

In fact, many of our clients transitioned from doing six figures to seven from the coaching, training and the work we were doing with them.

I am very grateful for the guidance and opportunity my business partner made available to me. After those seven years, we parted ways. That chance meeting in the water polo club had launched a prosperous partnership and consulting business we enjoyed together, and eventually, apart, as well.

I can attribute the following three progressive shifts within our business as key factors to our accelerated prosperity. These factors should be considered for every business.

The first one is to package and bundle up your services. We didn't offer just a one-hit wonder. It wasn't just a single transaction business. Offer a packaged service including support and additional products and services, all designed to deliver the best overall result and experience to your client.

I have helped many serviced-based businesses like

accountants to do exactly this; to go from the traditional model of trading hours or days for money to selling a choice of high-value, leveraged, ongoing service packages with monthly retainers. For the service-based business, this creates a higher transaction size and a more predictable cash flow; for their clients, it creates better outcomes and higher levels of service.

The second big lesson is to control the message you send out into the marketplace positioning yourself, or your business, as experts in your specific market.

The final shift comes through continually improving, developing and refining your sales process. Once refined, this process can be duplicated —and therefore, taught to other sales team members so you can have predictable sales results across your whole team.

Another bonus is the amazing intellectual property developed for a business as a direct result of combining the above.

A business with these systems in place also becomes more valuable.

In the next chapter, we loop back to when Blue Rocket was about to launch a franchised version of the consulting business, why we pulled the pin at the eleventh hour and how this almost wiped us out.

Learn from this near disaster so you can avoid the same mistake.

KEY LESSONS

1. In many businesses, 80 percent of revenue will come from only 20 percent of clients.
2. Creating a service package around your product or service will allow you to sell it for three times more than you could sell it for on its own.

If you'd like some help to implement this strategy in your service based business, you can enquire at www.john-blake.com.au

---

Chapter 10

Let's Franchise!

Having successfully built up our consulting business, naturally the idea of franchising the business came up in conversation.

The business had grown substantially using our business model and to grow bigger, we needed to create leverage. After in-depth discussions with my business partner, and then a franchise consultant, we decided to head down the path of franchising.

The process would be a long one as substantial changes to the laws surrounding franchising in Australia had recently been introduced. This was primarily due to the fact many franchisors had abused the system and taken money from unsuspecting investors, some of whom had bet their life savings and lost their homes.

Because of this, the franchise model itself had become strictly regulated. There was red tape, and a lot of paperwork to get through to become what the law called "franchise-ready."

We went through the entire process, which was almost eight months until we were franchise-ready. We had to complete stacks of documentation, navigate multiple legal hoops and endure a ton of accounting and structural changes to achieve this.

Let's Not

We were about to appoint our first franchisee, when a horrible layered realization came to us. The first was, if we were going to designate somebody to represent our brand, we needed to make sure that that person was a stellar candidate and the most shining-light success story we could produce. We needed to do this because the success of this first franchisee would pave the way for the growth of our entire franchise business.

The transition from being consultants and selling consultant services to now becoming franchisors and selling franchises, was a bigger leap and change than either of us could have expected.

Being in the selection process stage, we had seven interested candidates hoping for this opportunity and we were faced with the prospect of choosing the very best person. Problem was, neither of us had any faith in the ability of these candidates. We needed someone with a level of success already achieved in their field, and who also exuded a confidence to be able to execute our franchise model successfully.

The right fit was not delivered to us, so at the eleventh hour we made the difficult decision to pull the pin. We were literally, or metaphorically, all dressed up with nowhere to go. We had failed to address a key element in rolling out our product.

Many resources, including large chunks of our time and significant amounts of cash had been allocated to the process of franchising. The process had also caused us to take our focus off our core business which was of course, consulting.

And so, we decided not to go down the franchising path. What we did realize during this time however, was that we had begun to naturally operate two separate consulting businesses under one banner.

As there wasn't going to be any leverage from combining forces and we didn't have the potential to scale a franchise business, we realized it was a great time for us to go our separate ways and create independent consulting businesses in our niche markets.

I had learned so much from my business partner in terms of how to facilitate and set up a consulting business, and how to operate an effective training and coaching organization for which I am eternally grateful.

The takeaway? If you are going to start a partnership with someone, then there are a couple of things that must be considered. The first is that you obviously need to be compatible with that person. You're going to spend a lot of time with them, so it's imperative that you get along and are in alignment with each other's vision and expectations.

You also need to ensure you have a legal partnership agreement in place. In our situation, we had invested quite a large amount of money into a solid partnership agreement that accounted well for a scenario where one or both of us decided to leave the arrangement.

Thirdly, if you're going into partnership with someone, make sure it is with someone whose strengths will complement yours and vice versa. Your roles within the business need to be clearly defined by these strengths.

In the next chapter, I'd like to share with you how a devastating series of events exploded like a nuclear bomb, in the middle of my life and how I survived.

KEY LESSONS

1. If you start a partnership with someone, make sure you have a well thought out partnership agreement drawn up by a contract professional.
2. Never take your entire focus off your core business

To learn more go to www.highstakesselling.com

Chapter 11

Dream Life Shattered

Up until the business partnership dissolved, I had created, what in my mind, was a dream life.

Living in Margaret River I was surrounded by world-class waves, which being a surfing fanatic was fantastic. I had a beautiful beachside house, a gorgeous wife and was starting a young family. But all of this was about to come crashing down around me.

My son Lachie, was just six weeks old when my wife Shannon, started complaining of a sore back. We all thought it was because Lachie was such a big baby.

But the pain continued to worsen. Painkillers didn't make much difference and chiropractic and physio appointments couldn't relieve her pain.

She'd been to doctors but as her pain increased, we realized something was very wrong and we needed "second opinions."

You Have Six Months to Live

As it turned out, malignant melanoma tumors

leading on from a malignant skin cancer she'd had three years prior had spread into Shannon's lungs, liver, spine and brain. We were told the devastating news that she was terminal. She was given between six and nine months to live.

14 Weeks of Pure Hell

What ensued at that point in time was what I refer to as 14 weeks of pure hell. Shannon did not in fact even make it to six months, she passed away nine short weeks after her diagnosis.

It was devastating.

Aside from of course, dealing with the death of my wife of eight years, I was also left to look after two small children on my own. Lachie was five months old and Mischa was three and a half.

I knew I had to somehow put a structure in place to tend to my children so I could also continue working and running my business.

We were living in Margaret River, a three-hour drive from Perth, so my first priority was to move out of our house and closer to the city.

Because the decision had already been made to wind the partnership up prior to the passing of my wife, I had to also dissolve all the legal structures set up in the partnership and under the premise of operating a franchise business. Through this extremely challenging time I needed to launch a brand-new business under my own banner so as to continue to trade independently.

How to Close the Biggest Deal of Your Life While Emotionally Shattered

Fortunately, just prior to receiving Shannon's devastating diagnosis, I had had a meeting with a division of *The West Australian* newspaper. This was a lucrative client I wanted for my business and a signed agreement with them would be the biggest deal I would ever have closed.

I found out Shannon's results confirming her disease was, in fact, terminal as I was in the car driving to the meeting which would close this major deal with *The West Australian* newspaper.

Even though internally, I was absolutely shattered, somehow, I found the strength to operate efficiently. With all the intense emotional pressure I was under, I was able to secure one of the biggest deals of my life. It was, and still is, to this day, the hardest business meeting I have ever taken in my life.

Those 14 weeks taught me a lot. Lessons like: when you get put into a situation that emotionally ravages you, you become aware of how strong you can be.

When you're in a situation where you don't have any other alternative than to continue to be strong and to continue to make sure you're giving your best, you find an inner power. It's surprising how much resilience you can draw when going through a devastating event, from places you never knew existed inside you.

Lessons from Denichi

Through this incredibly dark time, I had been talking to my cousin. He is an intensely spiritual person, a black belt in tai chi, a black belt in the sword and he speaks fluent Japanese.

One time, I was explaining to him all these things that were happening to me and he said something I'll never forget. He said... "So, up until this all happened, things were going pretty well for you, weren't they?"

I said, "Yes, things were going great. I felt blessed with my good fortune, why?"

He said, "Well, it's inevitable." I said, "What do you mean it's inevitable?" He said, "Well, whenever things are going really, really well, you get tested." He continued, "But what's interesting about being tested is that you are never sent a test that you don't have the skills to be able to solve."

It was such a revelation. He then added, "Well, who better to deal with this than you? Who else do you know who would have the skill set to be able to deal with the enormity of this?"

To be honest, I didn't have an answer for him. I couldn't think of anybody who had done as much personal development work on themselves as I had.

It didn't take away my pain but it somehow gave me strength.

In the coming pages, you'll learn exactly how I transitioned through the recovery process both in my business as well as personally.

You will undoubtedly experience setbacks in your life and in business. Some of them will be minor and some of them may be major. It's how you move forward through them so as not to let these setbacks get the better of you.

What follows can be applied to almost any setback or upset you may face in your life or in your business. Most importantly, you will learn how to bounce back as quickly as possible from them.

KEY LESSONS

1. In both your business and your life you will have events and setbacks that will test you.
2. You are never sent a challenge or a setback that there isn't a solution for, or that you don't have the skills to be able to handle.

To learn more go to www.highstakesselling.com

Chapter 12

Recovery

After Shannon passed away, we moved closer to the city so we could get the support that we needed after such a tragic event. I needed to make sure the children were surrounded with love and attention as well, to allow me to continue to run my business and personally grieve.

I felt incredibly blessed that Shannon's parents, coupled with my own amazing parents, were and continue to be the most wonderful people. I can never thank any of them enough for how supportive they were during that time and how supportive they continue to be to this day with Lachie and Mishy.

It took a long time to come to grips with what had happened. In fact, there were many mornings where I woke up hoping that what had transpired had just been a nightmare. For months, I would wake up and think, *that was just a nightmare. I don't think this could really be happening.*

14 Steps to Getting Back on Track

It took me a long time to accept my new reality. But with time I felt things returning back to some sort of normality.

While dealing with Shannon's death I came up with these 14 steps to try to better wrap my head around the tragedy.

(If life right now is travelling along nicely for you, you may choose to skip this chapter and head to Chapter 13 and refer back to this if in the future, you ever need it. Whether it is through tragedy or just wanting to get yourself out of a rut, this 14-step guide may help.)

I originally wrote the following guideline as a blog and you can access it anytime at: www.highstakesselling.com

These are the 14 key steps I went through to weather what I now refer to as one of life's (un)perfect storms.

Number one is to deal with the reality of what is happening as it unfolds

When I was in the hospital and the specialist told us Shannon only had between six and nine months to live, I started dealing with the reality of what was going on. I started absorbing that I would be responsible for two small children, and that soon these small children would be adults and I would now be the one solely responsible to guide them throughout their life journey.

This started my internal dialogue, necessary to push me through the pain and into acceptance.

Intuitively, I knew the more I repeated that message to myself internally, the better prepared I would be for the inevitable. As I affirmed the facts to myself, the better I was able to get my head around it. From the moment we were told she was terminal, that her condition was not treatable, I had to start dealing with this new reality.

The second step is to find a positive amongst all the negatives.

And this is of course, by far the hardest step. When you lose your wife of eight years and your partner of ten, it's incredibly difficult to come up with anything positive.

This second step was torture to get past, but one I knew I had to work through. In doing so, I found I could move forward with some kind of hope for my life. There certainly wasn't a lot of things to be positive about at the time, but I managed to list a couple to work with.

One being that as I was now the sole parent in my children's lives, I would now have a bigger role to play. This wasn't much to be optimistic about, but focusing on my expanded role with my kids at times kept me going.

The third step is to gather information and dissect your options going forward.

Personally, I looked at many of the things I could do, also the things I needed to stop and things I needed to start doing. I looked at the option of doing nothing and looking after the children full-time, but for me this was absolutely not an option.

I looked at finishing up my business and getting a job somewhere, so I could possibly work shorter hours with less stress than running my own business. But the entrepreneur in me couldn't bring myself to get a job working for someone else. There was no way in the world I was going to roll over and let my circumstances dictate how I was going to deal with this event that had popped up in my life.

So, I chose to continue on in the consulting business and managed to make that year one of the biggest years I'd ever had. In fact, I did more in fees with everything I had going on than what I had done previously. I think the reason was because it was a good distraction.

The fourth stage is developing the knowledge and belief you can emerge better for the journey.

One of the lessons I came to understand from my

experience was that it could either totally disempower me, derail me and dictate the tone for the remainder of my life, or I could look at it as a snapshot in my life that could be turned into a positive—a tool that could aid in building my character and allow me to become more resilient.

Having the knowledge that you can emerge from such a tragic situation, or any setback for that matter, and knowing you can truly emerge better for the journey—it's a mighty acknowledgment.

The fifth step is locking into a course of action and holding your line.

Keep working at what you're going to do and stay pointed in the right direction. As long as you're progressing forward toward your goal and dreams you have momentum.

The sixth step is to seek help from others.

I was happy to accept help. Ask or you shall not receive and the worst that can happen is they can say no.

The seventh step requires you to say yes to all offers of help.

If someone says, "Oh, I'll look after the children for you," and you need some personal time to get away, take it! You need and deserve time out for you especially during trying times. I wouldn't necessarily take everybody up on it, but I was certainly grateful to accept many people's offers of help to get a bit of "me" time.

The eighth step is to simplify your life.

After Shannon passed, I sold property, extra cars and many things I just didn't need that were cluttering or impinging on my ability to recover. I simplified my life so it became as minimal an existence as possible.

The ninth step was to assume an identity avatar.

I personally identified with the phoenix, so much so, that I found a piece of art by comic artist, Todd McFarlane, which I likened to myself. You'll read more about this in a coming chapter.

For me, assuming an identity avatar gave me strength. Looking at my picture motivated me and inspired me.

Step ten is to assume a metaphor that encompasses your situation.

Throughout my ordeal, I likened my situation to a storm. What we know about a storm is that once the storm has passed, things become clear and calm again.

I continually redoubled my efforts to stay centered on that metaphor. I was like, "Okay, well, I'm in the middle of a storm. But I know at the end of the storm, there's going to be some blue water, some calm and some sunshine."

Step eleven is looking for some kind of humor in what's befalling you.

Again, this one is a fairly difficult task, but finding something to smile about in your circumstances is extremely important for maintaining balance. This could be as simple as your own forgetfulness.

Step twelve: know that we are never sent a challenge we can't deal with.

This one's critical to note and believe in and as you have already read, came into existence due to the conversation I had with my cousin.

Step thirteen is to reassess what's important to you.

Really take some time to work out what's important to you and what isn't important to you. When you have a life-changing event occur you start to realise certain things are no longer as important as they once seemed. This was a great step for me to go through.

Step fourteen is look after yourself and seek regular solitude in the activities you love.

Naturally, I created some space in my schedule to go surfing. It doesn't matter what it is you do, as long as you are happy in that moment.

So much of my recovery came down to making sure my internal dialogue was positive and productive. I also saw a psychologist to help me come out on the other side of the ruin and I found his help to be invaluable.

I talked to many people I trusted, too. Confiding in good people when you are in the thick of a catastrophe is important.

As much as I felt like every day I was strapping on heavy armor and going out to battle, in the end I emerged from it as well as could be expected, largely due to these 14 steps.

I wouldn't wish what happened to me on anyone, not even my worst enemy. But I think that these lessons really helped me and could also help you move through a situation, whether it be the death of a loved one or any setback in your life.

You can find these 14 steps any time at

Fast forward to present day and I am remarried to the most amazing woman I have ever met in my entire life, Tanya. My children now have an incredible mother they absolutely love and we all share an awesome family life I could never have imagined possible as I was going through the process of recovery. Which simply proves what I have believed all along: you CAN emerge better for the experience if you simply work toward that outcome.

In the next chapter, you'll learn more about my transition back to business on my terms and how two questions can help determine a new direction for you.

KEY LESSONS

1. The biggest part of dealing with any challenge is accepting the reality of the situation.
2. You are infinitely more resourceful and powerful than you may think you are when the situation demands that you get on and do what needs to be done, so you can keep moving.

To learn more go to www.highstakesselling.com

Chapter 13

Business on My Terms

When you create a set of rules for your business, and you're painfully deliberate in the way you conduct your company, it's not difficult to pull off what it is that you want out of your business.

After having gone through the initial drama of dealing with a new life with two children under the age of four, and a hell of a lot more pressure and responsibility on me, it took time to establish my ideal outcome.

Primarily, the way I needed to set up the business was to put a quarantine around my sanity. I did this to safeguard my ability to operate so I could still make the income I wanted to make, but I was profoundly strict on what I was doing.

The main objective for my resurrection was to decide my rules for what I wanted to do and also what I didn't want to do. Often the best way to find out what you want in your life and business is to ask yourself, "Okay, let's start with what I don't want."

Make a list of those things. It's easy to then flip them over, and focus on the positive equivalent for what you DO want.

For example, being a single parent, I didn't want to jump on any airplanes. My positive equivalent was that I was going to only work with clients in Perth. I didn't want to spend every single day of my week working with clients. That led to the choice that I would only do two client-facing days per week.

I only wanted a maximum of five clients at any given time. Each of those clients would be investing several thousand dollars per month to work with me. I was crystal clear on what I wanted and what I didn't want.

Time for surf and family. Yes, I wanted…and needed that.

I was infinitely sure of what I wanted. I had to be able to spend time with my family, to spend time surfing, to book no more than two client-facing days per week. I didn't want interstate travel for business, and I whittled down exactly how many clients I needed and about how much I wanted to earn from those clients per month.

It was an efficient and effective way to create the space I needed to move back into the business, but to move back into it on my terms. So, I would have the time and space to recover, which would allow me to do the things I wanted to do, while still running a successful business and helping my clients to achieve big breakthroughs in their sales.

In the next chapter, we get into how to apply the three key drivers for sales and business growth to develop your business into a prosperous success.

KEY LESSONS

1. Creating a business which operates under your lifestyle guidelines is the ultimate freedom.
2. Re-invention and resurrection need to happen regularly in your business if you are going to keep growing, improving and innovating.

To learn more go to www.highstakesselling.com

Chapter 14

Pillar 1: The Dream 100

When we started Blue Rocket, I was fortunate to have amassed over 10 years' worth of great relationships and contacts within the surfing industry.

These included relationships with companies I had both worked for and represented, retail clients I had sold product to, and for whom I had conducted specific product sales training, as well as a number of wholesalers I had become well acquainted with whom I had either worked for or become friends with.

As national sales manager of the sunglass company, I traveled interstate regularly throughout Australia plus travelled to America twice a year.

Because of this, I had developed a sizable and warm market of people I could contact and arrange to speak to regarding our new business.

When we originally set up Blue Rocket, it was primarily niched in the action sports or surf market, so we were almost inundated with companies we could work with.

Gradually, I worked my way through almost every single company in the surfing industry both in retail and wholesale.

For four years, we were kept very busy from my existing list of contacts.

It was fantastic. It worked. But after those golden years, the surf business transitioned into a mature market.

Warm Market Gone Cold

Suddenly, we found our niche market had gone cold and our contacts were leaving the surf clothing industry.

My business partner and I were now working on a new niche and direction we could move into.

We tried a variety of different things. We started to run more training events. We endeavored to make some of our products available online.

We found there was little we could do to give us the same deal flow we had experienced in the previous four years from our warm market, which had been made up primarily of repeat business and referrals.

We had tried some fax marketing and even done some cold calling. We attempted many different marketing methods to develop relationships with new people and companies we wanted to deal with.

We'd had some success with our marketing, but found the clients that were coming to us were less than our ideal clients. We would run online ads, or speak from the stage, and then get enquiries. But often, these leads didn't comprise the type of businesses we felt were optimal.

We needed to gain exposure from our marketing to attract dream clients in new industries, but our existing marketing was not reaching them.

By chance, I was listening to a program by Dan Kennedy one day. He talked about the idea of creating a pack of information that you could send to a potential client. Doing so, would establish credibility prior to even executing the first contact with them.

The Contact Power Pack

The pack he spoke of included a book, or a free report written by the business. It would also contain an audio program, perhaps an interview and some video testimonials on a DVD.

A business would add into the packet, a list of frequently asked questions and other education-based marketing pieces of information, that were designed to position them as an expert. Because of this expert educator positioning, you would also be preconditioning your potential client prior to even speaking to them.

I listened to it all on audio. I didn't attend any of his trainings. I didn't see the video side of what he was doing. I just listened as he described what it was he would put together and how it worked.

I started doing what he recommended for our business. The first thing we did was to decide what we were going to include in our package. Then we started to market our business by sending these packages to people in decision making roles.

As a result, we started to connect with some bigger clients that would have been unlikely to come to us through our prior marketing efforts. We had shown up differently to our competitors who were still cold calling or cold emailing. We introduced ourselves with good information and as the experts and so established authority and a good connection.

Consequently, we were then able to get through to the decision makers on the phone, and make appointments so we could have a real conversation about the possibility of working together.

In the coming chapters, I'll explain more about how to go direct to your dream clients, and what to include in your package.

We Called That List "The Dream 100"

I learned about The Dream 100 from another gentleman I had studied under, Chet Holmes. Sadly, he passed away a couple of years ago. He was extraordinarily brilliant as it related to simply encouraging people to go after a better pedigree of client.

We would look and see who was advertising. We would also check out the weekend magazines included with the paper.

We would also go online to see which companies were advertising for salespeople, because typically, if people were advertising for staff, it meant their business was growing. If their business was growing, then they would likely need more systemization, training and more scalability.

We built a strong list of 100 companies we wanted to do business with. We researched who the decision makers were and how their companies were performing.

We would then put packages together and send them to those targets we had identified as being potential strong leads.

For this effort, we were able to get in front of key clients with high turnover and teams of salespeople who were an ideal fit for our services.

Walking in on Your Own Project

Because we were positioning ourselves with these packages so cleverly as experts in sales consulting, on a couple of occasions we would get meetings with potential clients, and because of what we had sent them, and because of how powerful it was, they had already made the decision to engage our services prior to our arrival.

It was almost like walking in on your own project that had started without you.

I have now introduced and implemented the Dream 100 process to over 80 of my clients, and they are enjoying spectacular results.

The Dream 100 is one of the strongest strategies for success I have experienced both within my own business, as well as for businesses I have worked with; it occurs simply by working out exactly who you want to work with.

When combined with the Contact Power Pack, it becomes an incredibly powerful tool to use to rapidly increase your penetration with target clients.

Because most companies don't have an actual strategy to get in front of their dream clients, other than cold calling and cold emailing, they often don't obtain clients ideal to them.

Firstly, identify your dream clients, then give information that is valuable to them, that also positions you as the expert.

In the next chapter, I guide you on information and ideas that need to be considered for your Contact Power Pack, how to control your message to your market and how to position yourself as your prospect's logical choice, all while you warm them up until they are ready to buy.

KEY LESSONS

1. Creating a Dream 100 list of the clients you would ideally love to work with is one of the most productive things you can do.
2. Controlling what your client knows about you before your first call using the Contact Power Pack allows you to get in front of clients quickly and easily.

To learn more go to www.highstakesselling.com

Chapter 15

Pillar 2: Education-Based Marketing

One of the important lessons learnt through studying with Chet Holmes was the idea of education-based marketing. This concept makes great sense when you consider the market for any product.

The Market for Any Product

If you envision a triangle, and you slice the triangle into five different horizontal slices, at the very tip top of the triangle, are the three percent of any market buying right now.

Picture it this way: if you walk into a room of 100 randomly selected people, and you were to say, "Who in this room needs a new refrigerator right now?" about three people are going to put their hands up.

If you were to then say, "Put your hand up if you are in the market for a refrigerator. Maybe your existing refrigerator is on the way out and you are shopping around for a new one?" Another seven hands would go up.

The next section below on the triangle represents

the 30 percent of potential customers who are open to the idea of buying a refrigerator. They're not necessarily in the market at that exact moment, but they're open to the idea.

If you were to then separate the remaining bottom of the triangle with another horizontal line, you would have the 30 percent of people who are not thinking about buying a new refrigerator. What's left is the section at the bottom: the remaining 30 percent who think they don't need a new refrigerator.

In this way, you've represented 100 percent of the market. You've got the three percent buying now, the seven percent who are in the market. Underneath that, you've got the 30 percent who are open to purchase. Underneath that section, the 30 percent who aren't thinking about it. Finally, down at the bottom of the triangle, you've got the 30 percent who don't think they need a new refrigerator at all.

THE MARKET FOR ANY PRODUCT

- 3% buying now
- 7% in the market
- 30% open to it
- 30% not thinking about it
- 30% think they don't need it

What we realize when we look at normal targeted marketing is it's almost all aimed at the three percent of the market who are buying right now, and sometimes, the seven percent underneath, who are in the market.

Check out the marketing you see for companies trying to sell televisions: let's say they advertise 36 months' interest-free. Well, if you're not in the market for a television, you are probably not going to take advantage of that offer, unless you've got somewhere else in your house where you want to put a television. In short, if you are not in the market, you probably wouldn't take them up on their offer.

Most of the marketing you see is aimed at the top three percent or the top ten percent of the market. Which is why the need for education-based marketing is relevant, especially when you consider there are people who will be open to the idea of having a refrigerator or buying something, but they're probably just not ready to buy right now.

What you have the opportunity to do, through this alternative marketing, is develop a relationship with those people. Even if it's the 30 percent of the people who are open to the idea or not thinking about it; you can compel and get their attention by offering information to them that is of interest, even if they are not buying now or in the market.

If I were to use my own businesses for example, one of the most popular pieces of education-based marketing that we ever created was a free report outlining the four most costly mistakes companies can make when they train their sales team.

As a business owner, this information would be of interest to you, regardless of whether you are in the market to train your sales team right now, or if you were thinking about doing it in six, or twelve months' time. When you use education-based marketing, you capture the attention of a larger percentage of the market.

Impartial Versus Pitchy

When you implement this idea, you can come across as impartial, because it's not a product pitch. You're not pushing your brochure with a whole bunch of product in there. You're essentially giving businesses or potential clients useful information that can help them in their business or life that they often aren't aware of.

Market Data

You want to ideally create three "ahas," or bring three points to your prospects' attention that they probably don't know about. The best way to do this is using market data. For example, in my business, if I were creating some education based marketing for a retailer, I could use market data that explains that 82 percent of lost sales are lost in the initial customer approach.

One piece of market data I would use with a target client who focuses on business-to-business sales, is that 44 percent of salespeople give up after the first time they follow up with a prospect who hasn't purchased.

Education-based marketing content can be used on

social media as well. It can be used on your website. And it can also be used in free reports you market digitally.

Showing Up Differently

Education-based marketing is certainly not a new concept. There are many different people and lots of companies using it. The difference is, with our education-based marketing we package it up and put it in hard copy.

So, we put together a package, which contains a hard copy free report and an audio CD recording in a DVD case with a cover letter. Then we send this to the Dream 100 targets we have identified.

There are many people using digital marketing in today's world to get to their dream clients, however, that digital pathway is in gridlock.

It's challenging to get through to someone who doesn't know you, using email. It's challenging to get through to people in any digital context because there are just so many messages trying to find their way through to them. A lot of companies and highly important people, who are too busy, use gatekeepers, executive assistants and personal assistants to filter these digital messages for them. So, often your messages will never even reach them.

Taking Up Space on Their Desk

When you send something that looks impressive, that's presented well and takes up physical space on someone's desk, you'll find that people will look at it and are also unlikely to throw your material out. You will have your target's attention.

In the coming chapters, I'll talk more about the direct-to-corporate strategy and provide some real-life examples that have worked. What I will also share with you is a potent method that has proven to get you in front of higher end target clients.

There are many people using this precise strategy to market their business online both through social media and on their websites. However, not many people are using it offline, in hard copy in a direct play to get in front of their dream clients—those clients who they would ideally love to work with. I'm talking about the clients who aren't gravitating to them through existing marketing efforts.

In the next chapter, I'm going to talk about why it is imperative to have a proven sales process in place to convert higher numbers of your enquiries. I'll also expand on the direct-to-corporate strategy and how it works in conjunction with the education-based marketing package.

KEY LESSONS

1. Education-based marketing allows you to become an educator to your target client.
2. Education-based marketing allows you to shift your client's buying criteria away from price and support value-based buying decisions.

To learn more go to www.highstakesselling.com

Chapter 16

Why You <u>Need</u> a Sales Process

Over the past 12 years as a sales coach, consultant and trainer, I have read hundreds of books and listened to numerous audio programs on sales. I have attended many trainings on sales, and have taken online training from many of the most well-known sales coaches and sales education experts in the world.

Couple that with the successful collation, application and testing of this training, and I have produced a sales process that when used with potential clients, creates an environment where they will be more likely to make a "yes" purchasing decision with you.

Why Have a Sales Process?

People sometimes ask why a business should have a sales process and it's a good question. I mean why can't we just talk to potential customers? Won't the ones who are interested just sign up anyway?

Well there are few key reasons for this...

Product Dump Mode

The first one is that in the absence of having a sales process, most salespeople simply go into product dump mode. Meaning, they simply recite the features and advantages of their product and in doing so, think they are selling. Nothing could be further from the truth. Don't get me wrong, knowing your product is important and speaking about it at the right time in the process is important as well, but you should not do this until you've thoroughly found out about your client and what it is that they need.

Roller Coaster Results

If there is no predictable sales process, what you typically get is roller coaster results. If you or your team are simply order taking and not using a predictable process, the results will rarely, if ever be consistently good.

Too Reliant on One Person

I have literally seen businesses held at ransom by one salesperson who is the one bringing in 80 percent of the revenue or a successful business that is completely reliant on the owner of the business for the majority of its sales. Naturally, this leaves the business vulnerable because if that person leaves or gets sick, the business will almost definitely suffer.

Can't Scale or Grow

Ultimately, this also means the business can't scale up or grow either.

Proper Diagnostics

A great sales system allows you to properly diagnose a potential client's situation to determine the best course of action for them, or ultimately, if you want them as a client in the first place.

Consistent Results

Having an effective sales process in place that has been refined and proven means you will receive consistent, predictable results across the board to grow your sales and your business.

Everyone Winning

A strategic sales process allows all your salespeople to get consistent results, too, which means the whole sales team and the whole business will win.

This ultimately allows you to grow and scale your business systematically.

The Conversion Ladder

There are five levels on the conversion ladder that occur in businesses, ranging from companies that have no sales process in place, to businesses that have a proven, tested and refined sales process. Below are the results you can typically expect at each level as you move up.

No Sales Process

Businesses that have no sales process in place typically convert around 5-10 percent of their enquiries into sales. Interestingly, some businesses can actually make their numbers work from this conversion rate, but as you can imagine they are doing a stack of extra work for a lesser return.

Ineffective

The businesses in this category have the resemblance of a sales process, but it's either largely ineffective with its conversions or the sales team have a loose understanding and weak grasp of it. These businesses can typically expect around 10-15 percent conversion.

Generic

These businesses typically use a sales process, but it's one they have usually learned from a book or a seminar that is generally not catered toward their specific product or service offer. A generic process is certainly better than not having one at all and these businesses typically convert at around 15-30 percent.

To compare, the average business benchmark for most businesses is a 20-25 percent successful conversion rate.

Structured

These businesses have a sales process that is structured toward their specific industry, market and product. These businesses have developed a process that works and they can expect a 30 to sometimes even 60 percent conversion rate from the enquiry to becoming a paying client.

Proven, Tested and Refined

Once a business has a sales process in place and it's working, it is critical they continue to improve it by testing it and implementing ongoing coaching with the team members who are using it.

By continuing to test and refine your process, businesses over time, can expect to grow their conversions from 60 percent to between 80 and 90 percent.

Now think about that for a moment.

The same investment paid into their advertising and marketing, the same overheads and running costs but a result that can double and triple your profit.

To a company, business owner or commission salesperson, this increase is massive.

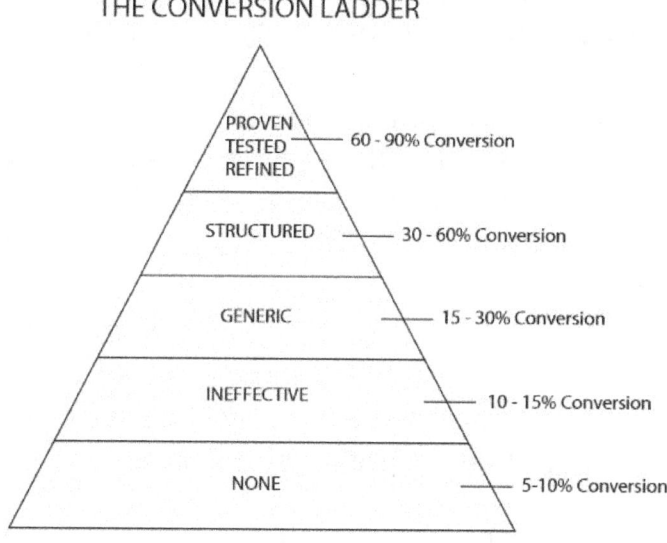

THE CONVERSION LADDER

From 40-90 Percent Sales Conversions

I worked on a sales process for a client in the health and wellness industry.

Her business went from consistently converting 4 out of 10 enquiries to, after working on her sales process, converting 8-9 out of every 10 enquiries into paying clients.

The work we have done together has totally transformed her business. Her profit has gone through the roof and she is now not only paying chunks off her business loan, she has built up her bank accounts to grow and protect her business, and also reward her team with many more benefits.

And what's even better, she has now trained other team members to use the same process, gaining the same predictable conversion rate, so she now has a freedom within her business she did not have before.

In the next chapter, you'll learn the exact framework I use with clients to create a proven, refined sales process that delivers predictable results.

If you would like me to help you develop a sales framework for your sales team, specific to your business, contact me through my website at www.john-blake.com.au

KEY LESSONS

1. Companies with no sales process have little scope to grow as they are often too reliant on one person or very low conversion rates.
2. Having a structured sales process in place can allow a business to double their profits without increasing any other expenses.
3. Having a refined, proven, tested process in place can produce conversion rates of up to 80-90 percent.

To learn more go to www.highstakesselling.com

Chapter 17

Creating Your STRIKE Sales Framework

The STRIKE sales framework is a foundation and structure for building your sales process

S	**Situation**
T	**Troubleshooting**
R	**Results**
I	**Impact**
K	**Kick Start**
E	**Enroll**

1. Situation – Assessing your client's situation

The first part of the conversation you need to lead your contact through will assess their situation. Various factors make up your assessment of a client. Contextually, you are talking to somebody who, in many ways, doesn't know you particularly well, or at all, and they are just coming into a sales conversation.

Prospects tend to have certain preconceptions about what happens in sales conversations. They tend to have also experienced negative interactions with salespeople in their past.

Some salespeople they've dealt with may have been

rude or pushy. Some prospects have been told negative things about salespeople from their parents or from teachers as they've grown up.

Whether in a business situation or as a paying customer, people may have baggage around a sales conversation. That's why in the first part of a sales process, we need to acknowledge the situation that exists for them. We can do this in a few different ways. First, we need to create rapport with the person we're talking to and try to find a point in common with them.

Notice I say a "point in common" rather than advising to ask about their interests. Establishing a point in common means you can both talk sincerely and authentically about a topic you BOTH share an interest in which can create rapport between you. Rapport can typically revolve around...

Family – For example if you both have children.
Occupation – Jobs or industries you may both have worked in.
Recreation – What you do on the weekends, e.g., fishing.
Nationality – The country or part of the country where you grew up.

You also need to create an agenda of what is going to happen in your conversation.

The best way to create an agenda is to FRAME the conversation.

Framing creates a non-threatening expectation around what will happen in the conversation. If it's done correctly, it establishes credibility, control and authority.

An example of a frame that can be used at the start of a sales conversation could be: "So, I can work out if I can help you or not, I have a few questions to go through with you and I was going to take a few notes as we go. Is that Okay?"

2. Troubleshooting – establish your prospect's core motivation or problem

The second thing we need to do is establish our prospect's core motivation or core problem and why they have come to us. Most people—in fact, around 70 percent—will make their purchasing decision to solve a problem.

About 30 percent will make a purchasing decision to improve their situation. If 70 percent of people make a purchasing decision to solve a problem, we need to identify the problem. The troubleshooting part defines the motivation behind the purchase, or the problem they are looking to solve.

One of the best ways to identify the core motivation

or problem behind the purchase is to simply ask, "What made you decide to contact us today?" or "What made you decide to come in and see us today?"

The response you'll get is typically going to be the core motivation or "trigger" behind why they contacted you. This will, in most cases, reveal the problem they are trying to solve.

Once your client has shared the problem they want to solve, we then need to "shine a light" on that problem.

This typically involves asking your potential client to explain in more detail about the problem they have shared with you and how it is impacting them.

The reason we want to do this, is when our client talks in more detail about the problem or motivation behind the purchase, it expands in importance in their mind.

When the problem or motivation expands in their mind, it becomes large enough to a point where they realize the cost of doing nothing becomes greater than the cost of investing in your product or service. It is in that moment, that a sale is most likely to take place.

In summary **"A purchase takes place FIRST, in**

the mind of our client ONLY when the perceived cost of doing nothing becomes greater than the investment in your product or service."

3. The Result – the result they are wanting from contacting or seeing you

Next, we need to find out what the result is that they are expecting from your product or service. What is the picture they have in their head? What is the outcome they are looking for by making their purchase?

4. Impact – how will the outcome impact their lives?

In step four, we need to go deeper and look at what specifically will be different in their world as a direct result of making their purchasing decision. We must also show the impact of doing nothing and the monetary cost of doing nothing, so they can see the truth of why they need to make a change to their situation.

It is imperative to do this.

We then need to ask our prospect, "Okay, what would life look like in a scenario where this is fixed, where after this purchase has been made, your situation has changed for the better?" We must show both sides of the coin.

When we've proven the positive impact or cost of working with us and discussed the negative impact of taking no action, it's only then that we can come in with our solution to produce the result the prospect has concluded they themselves, now need.

One of the biggest mistakes salespeople make is they start a conversation where they immediately talk about their product, or their solution, without having properly diagnosed the client's situation and requirements.

5. Kick-Start the Solution – apply your solution to their problem/desire

It's only once we have acknowledged the context of the conversation, that we can help the person to relax. Once we've then found out what the problem is, and found out what the person's hoping for in terms of results we'll know how it will impact their world. It's only at this point that we then can insert our customized solution into the conversation. We have kick-started the solution for them. We then want to walk them through what will happen when we roll out the plan to resolve their problem or fill their need.

6. Enrolling – confirm the sale

The last part is enrolling our prospect into

confirming the sale and placing the order. This step could also take the form of setting the next appointment, or scheduling the next conversation.

If you're in a conversation with somebody, and you must go back and prepare a proposal, or the person needs to go and do a couple of things in order for them to be able to make that purchase, one of the best things you can do is simply confirm the next step of the process.

Confirming the Next Step of the Process

What is the next part of the process that needs to happen? In most cases, this will be a conversation. Go ahead and ask your prospect who hasn't confirmed their choice, "When would you like to continue the conversation?" Because that will then give you a specific time, on a specific day, that you can ring them and move the sale forward.

Sometimes, the next step involves merely getting your prospect to do what they need to do to make the purchase. Sometimes, you can get your prospect to the next step by saying something like, "All I need you to do is complete this paperwork, so we can get you set up in our system, and then we can get started next week."

You might also try, "What needs to happen next is I need you to complete this document here, and put your autograph down at the bottom. We can then get you set up in our system and begin your training on how to use the software," or "We can start the process of building your new house." Whatever the case may be.

Many salespeople get caught up in the closing part of the process, but what they don't realize is you must get the first part, or the first 80 percent of the sales conversation right, so the last part of the conversation is simple. It should be a logical easy transition for your prospect to say yes to the sale, or to confirm the next step going forward.

Typically, if you find yourself having to handle objections or really pushing someone hard to close the sale, it means you haven't refined the front end of your sales process properly.

As an example, I had a call from a lady who wanted me to mystery shop the salesperson they had appointed to take calls for a dog obedience franchise. I rang the sales lady and pretended I had a Jack Russell who was misbehaving.

She didn't take me through a process similar to what I have outlined, finding out the specific problem I was experiencing with my dog.

Instead of asking me what the result was that I was looking for and how that result would change things for me, this sales lady went straight into a long-winded explanation about their amazing product.

Sure, she did a fine job explaining the product, what it did and how good it was, but it had no relevance to my situation, because she hadn't found out enough about what it was that I was looking for and most importantly the outcome I was seeking.

Because of this, the description of her service was irrelevant to my "imaginary" circumstances.

I later found out her conversion rate was only 10 percent, which, when you consider the fact she handled thousands of dollars' worth of leads every day for all the franchise owners, meant she was wasting a ton of money in lost sales and the marketing dollars spent generating the enquiries.

If you'd like to watch a detailed explanation of the STRIKE sales process, I offer a video online. Simply go to: **www.highstakesselling.com**

In the next chapter, I'll take you through a highly effective direct-to-corporate formula that can be used to connect with the key decision makers in your dream client list who aren't finding their way to you through your existing marketing channels.

KEY LESSONS

S – Situation
T – Troubleshooting
R – Results
I – Impact
K – Kick Start
E- Enroll

To learn more go to www.highstakesselling.com

Chapter 18

The Direct-to-Corporate Formula

We've already discovered the elements of the Contact Power Pack, and explored education-based marketing. Now, we need to put the direct-to-corporate formula into place for you.

Step One: Who is Your Dream Client?

Take some time to sit down and work out exactly who it is you would ideally love to have as a client. I've found the best way to do this is to take the top two or three clients in your portfolio and then ask yourself, *if I had a magic wand and I could duplicate these clients, what would I duplicate about them?*

Then look at where defining elements and aspects of those clients intersect. It might be that you have discovered the business owner needs to be between the ages of thirty-five and forty-five. It might be that your dream client needs to have a minimum turnover of $X.

It may be that they need to sell a product with a high profit margin. They might need to be in a market that's expanding. Each of these components can help you to determine who your dream clients are.

Step Two: Creating Your Dream 100

Next, look in different places where you can find your dream clients. Places may include;

- Yellow pages
- Web directories
- Newspapers
- Magazines
- LinkedIn
- Databases
- Business publications
- Driving through industrial areas
- Online job boards
- Target market blogs
- Target market Facebook pages and groups
- Referrals

What you want is to start off with a list of between 100 and 150 prospects. You then refine that list by doing research on each of them.

If you're sending somebody a package of information, you're investing quite a lot of time and money constructing, and delivering that information. If you're sending them an audio program or a free report, you need to make sure you can hedge your bets to some extent, so that you are a good fit for that business.

You need to work out whether it's worth sending your valuable information to those prospects.

Step Three: Fine-Tune Your List

Over the years, one of the criteria I've used in deciding who I do business with, revolves around the fact I live in Perth. As I move through the prospecting process, I discover if a potential client has a head office in Perth or if I will have to fly over to the east coast of Australia to get a buying decision. Through research, I must decide if it's a viable decision to send them a pack and open the lines of discussion. I must base this decision on the size of the company and their sales team or their turnover and average transaction size.

Another example of refining a list is, I had a client who was selling photocopiers. He made a list of a hundred people he wanted to deal with. He started to refine his list when I said to him, "Ring up and ask them one, if they have a photocopier. two, how long they've had the photocopier and three, if they're happy with it."

If they answer, "Yes, we have a photocopier. Yes, we've had it for three years. No, we're not happy with it," then they are probably a great candidate to receive a direct package from you.

Step 4: Send Them Your Pack

The pack needs to be ideally sent in an express post pack or through a courier because it will get to the decision maker faster. It will cut through the clutter.

It also needs to come with a well written cover letter. The cover letter should be written in a strategic way. In particular, your cover letter should read that you're going to contact them within a particular time frame.

You can download a free cover letter template at **www.highstakesselling.com**

Step 5: Call Them

Make sure you call them within the timeframe you've listed on that cover letter.

When you call, your objective is to have a conversation with them on the phone. A couple of things can happen.

1) You're not going to get ahold of them. Some people, you just won't reach. It's as simple as that.

2) You're going to get through to them, but that moment may not be ideal for them to speak with you. So, you will need to politely arrange a time to call when it's more convenient for them.

3) You are going to speak with them, and schedule an appointment.

If you want to go into greater depth with this signature system, you can go to **www.john-blake.com.au**, where I have posted my program that walks you through exactly what it is that you need to do from the very beginning.

You can also learn how to create an effective marketing campaign using the Contact Power Pack guidelines. You'll also learn how to convert your prospect using the STRIKE sales framework once you're in front of them.

Step 6: The Follow Up

From here, download my book *How to Follow Up Without Being a Stalker* at:

www.john-blake.com.au.

This book will walk you through the follow up process, including the implementation of voicemail and email templates, as well as outlining how often and when to email your prospects.

You'll also learn what to say during phone calls, and how long to keep following up with them, so they won't feel like you're overstepping the mark or stalking them.

In the next chapter, I'll go into how you can use effective follow up strategies to cash in on the lucrative opportunities most salespeople miss, all due to poor or inconsistent follow up.

KEY LESSONS

1. The digital road to your dream client is in gridlock.
2. The offline path to them is empty.
3. Going direct to your dream client is easy if you use a proven system to get their attention prior to contact.

To learn more go to www.highstakesselling.com

Chapter 19

The Follow Up

One of the biggest areas of lost sales, and an area it would be absolutely remiss for me not to include in this book, is following up. There is a huge cost associated with generating leads. Recent data specifying how leads are often handled is particularly alarming when you consider in some cases, it can cost a company between $400 and $1,500 per lead to generate.

How Most Salespeople Handle Follow Up

Leads are often handled poorly, as I've previously shown. It is shocking to me to know the statistic that 44 percent of salespeople give up after one follow-up. This statistic is based around a potential client who has enquired who hasn't taken any action toward purchasing. What's also intriguing to note, is 80 percent of sales are made after the *fifth follow up*. That's a whole lot of unbanked business revenue left on the table.

Why Salespeople Give Up Way Too Early

When I ask salespeople, "Why do you give up? Why haven't you called that person back?" I tend to get answers, like, "I don't want to be seen as pushy," and "I don't want to be a stalker. If they wanted to go ahead, they would contact me."

You Jump on and off Their Radar

The reality is that each buyer has a set of priorities in their life, and the things on the top of that list tend to go up and down. Think of a client's priorities as a radar.

One week, buying your product or service might be on the top of the priority list and so you are on their radar as a little green dot without many other priorities dotted around you. But within two or three days, that list can totally change. What was highly important earlier on in the week, or even earlier on in the month, could be way, way down their list of priorities now. Suddenly, you are nowhere to be seen on the radar and you may not reappear for a while.

An Example in Home Security Sales

Many salespeople tend to give up, but they give up for the wrong reasons. An example of this involves a client who sells security systems for people's homes. When I began working with his business, I said to his team, "Put your hand up if, after you go and see a person with a quote to put a security system in their home, you follow up with that person once."

The four reps in the room all put their hands up. I said, "Put your hand up if you follow up twice." None of the hands went up. I said, "Put your hand up if you follow up more than twice." No hands went up. Then I instructed, "What I want you to do is, over the next two weeks, call every single person you've seen in the last 90 days, who you've done a quote for, but who haven't bought a security system yet."

Two weeks went by, and we all sat back in the room again. I said, "Okay. So…what happened?" All four reps had made a minimum $7,000 sale, simply by following up with people who had enquired, who'd had a quote done, but who hadn't bought.

This is a classic example of when people don't buy, and it's not for the reasons salespeople and business owners think. When I asked those reps what the reasons were their prospect hadn't bought prior to their follow up, one of them answered, "My customer said, 'Oh, I've been in America, and so I haven't listened to my telephone messages or read my emails yet.'"

Another one said, "My daughter broke her leg. We've been in total lockdown for the last month, because we've been trying to get everything sorted and get her fixed up and back to school." It was a similar case for the other two reps, and *the reason the customers hadn't yet bought had zero to do with the salesperson.* The best part? Every single one of those customers had said, "Thank you so much for calling me back."

What we also know is that 50 percent of people who enquire about a product or service may take up to 18 months to finalize their decision to buy.

Three Years of Follow Up to Land One Client Worth Millions

Another example is the business agreement signed with *The Western Australian* newspapers. What I didn't mention earlier in the book is that deal took three years to close. That's right. I followed up with that client for three years straight, (including the initial contact with the sales director using the Contact Power Pack) during which time they also went through two sales managers and two general managers. We finally arrived to a time where they were ready to continue a conversation about doing a deal with Blue Rocket.

As our business partnership was ending at the time, we split this account. I took the whole of the West Australian Regional Newspapers while my business partner worked with *The West Australian* newspaper account. In total, that account ended up being the biggest we secured during our time at Blue Rocket and all because we had persisted and finally won the business.

It is possible to follow up systematically, professionally and efficiently with a contact until they are ready to buy. Employing a systematic way to follow up means eventually you will reach a segment of people who will make a purchase from you. That's why following up is such an important part of the sales process.

In the next chapter, I'm going to share with you my biggest lessons I've learned from 28 years in sales and how to help you with coaching that can keep you on a direct path to success.

KEY LESSONS

1. When clients don't respond it's almost never about you.
2. 50percent of buyers will make a purchase within 18 months of their initial enquiry.
3. Only 15-20 percent will purchase in the first 90 days.
4. Most businesses and salespeople leave a fortune on the table because they don't follow up.

To learn more go to www.highstakesselling.com

Chapter 20

Key Lessons, and Where to From Here?

In closing, if I were to share some of the biggest lessons I have learned in 28 years of sales, the first would be to back yourself!

In many situations, you are going to be faced with a choice as to whether to retreat or whether to advance. This could simply be making another call. It could be following up with somebody who hasn't purchased. It could be going back to a contact you've made a recommendation to, but who hasn't made any moves yet.

Many times, I've looked at what I have to do, and the choices I need to make. One of the approaches that has always served me well is to move toward the side of being bold and to back myself, rather than withdrawing.

It's such an important part of sales and selling, and it will consistently keep you on your path to success. Ask yourself: 1) What is it I need to do? 2) How many calls do I need to make? 3) Who do I need to meet?

Are Salespeople Born or Can They Be Created?

One of the main reasons I do what I do, is based around the question that asks whether salespeople are born, or whether salespeople can be made? It's the age-old "nurture versus nature" argument.

My opinion of this is that there are certain people who have a predisposition for selling. There are people who, for whatever reason, possess a certain personality type that lends them to succeed at selling. As embarrassing as this may be, I am not one of those people.

In the psychometric tests I have taken (and there are plenty of psychometric tests for salespeople), I have skewed toward "introvert."

Links to a handful of these tests are available in the resources section at the front of this book. I've also included information on the DISC profile, which is another psychological assessment you can read about to see where your personality falls.

With the psychometric tests that relate specifically to salespeople, my results always show up as being somebody who doesn't necessarily have a predisposition for selling. For someone who teaches about selling, this might sound a bit strange; however, what I do know is this, anyone who can follow a system, who has a willingness to become better at selling, can achieve success in selling.

My own experience is that I don't believe I am a natural-born salesperson. I'm somebody who had a willingness to do it, who sought the training and the instruction and who has gathered experience along the way. It has allowed me to earn an excellent living, and to achieve a level of success I am proud of.

If you do have the right attitude and if you have the willingness to learn, you can become a stellar example of sales success.

My Ongoing Mission

My ongoing mission is to empower people to create conversations that don't feel like sales conversations or heavy pitching, but instead result in the potential client becoming a paying client—because it feels good to them by doing so.

Where to From Here?

In terms of going forward, I would recommend attending my 1 Day Professional Sales Master Class, where I cover my entire curriculum for controlling your message, connecting with your ideal prospects and converting them into paying clients.

As I work with my clients, we focus on three outcomes:

...Controlling your Message so your potential clients see you as the very best option. This also warms people up until they are ready to do business with you...

...Converting higher numbers of leads and enquiries into paying clients at the fees you want to charge (without having to use any sales pressure or weirdness)...

...Connecting with dream clients and referral partners who can send you large numbers of clients…

I've got a complete system I go through with my clients over the course of 12 months. Instead of spending a year, we cut your learning curve and spend a full day together, giving you the entire curriculum for doubling or even tripling your sales revenue.

The page that explains the day's agenda can be found at:

http://john-blake.com.au/1-day-professional-sales-master-class/

You can register your seats at this link:

https://johnblake.clickfunnels.com/order

If you don't live in Perth or can't travel to Perth, I also offer a digital version of this training, which you can access through my website:

www.john-blake.com.au.

I also offer a 12-month program called The Conversion Mastery Program. In this program, we continually refine and improve three areas in your business: the way you are controlling your message, the way you are connecting with your dream clients and your dream referral partners who have the potential to send you large sums of business. We also cover how to continually refine your conversion process, so as to consistently convert more enquiries into paying clients. We also build your customized Connect Power Pac for getting the attention and getting in front of your dream clients.

The Conversion Mastery Program is designed to double your conversion rates and triple the size of your businesses. This is achieved through the constant refinement of your offer and controlling your message and sales process. If the Conversion Mastery Program appeals to you, please go to:

www.john-blake.com.au.

I would like to thank you so much for purchasing this book. It's my sincere hope that through the examples, stories and frameworks I've shared with you, it will help you build a successful career in sales which will allow you the lifestyle you want and all the success you've ever dreamed of.

About the Author

Over the past 28 years, John Blake has been a successful salesperson, sales manager, business owner, author and sales coach and mentor.

John is obsessed with helping business people explode their sales results using a unique process that empowers both his clients and their clients whilst being 100 percent sincere and avoiding dated, clichéd sales approaches.

By age 26, whilst national sales manager of a recognised, international sunglass distributor for Australia and Asia, John played a key role in growing sales from a modest $750,00 per year to a whopping $6M per year in turnover in just three years.

Over the last 10 years, John's proven formula for cracking open the vault to unlock huge sales increases has been applied to hundreds of businesses spanning numerous industries.

John's approach is unique because EVERY sales strategy and idea you'll learn has been thoroughly road tested and proven by his own experiences FIRST.

The three main problems John solves for his clients are low conversion rates, low transaction sizes and an inability to engage with and convert premium clients.

John's clients typically experience a faster sales cycle and boosted confidence in their sales teams, which means a more enjoyable, profitable experience for both his clients and their customers.

Whilst consulting, some of the companies in his portfolio have included Westfarmers Insurance, Oakley, Rip Curl, The West Australian Regional Newspaper Group, Decor Blinds & Curtains, CINEads, RAC, Vantage Performance, and Stocker Preston Real Estate, to name just a few.

www.ingramcontent.com/pod-product-compliance
Lightning Source LLC
Chambersburg PA
CBHW061439180526
45170CB00004B/1473